Penguin Critical
Advisory Edito

William Shakespe

A Midsummer Night's Dream

Peter Hollindale

Penguin Books

To Philip and Nicholas
with love

PENGUIN BOOKS

Published by the Penguin Group
Penguin Books Ltd, 27 Wrights Lane, London W8 5TZ, England
Penguin Books USA Inc., 375 Hudson Street, New York, New York 10014, USA
Penguin Books Australia Ltd, Ringwood, Victoria, Australia
Penguin Books Canada Ltd, 10 Alcorn Avenue, Toronto, Ontario, Canada M4V 3B2
Penguin Books (NZ) Ltd, 182–190 Wairau Road, Auckland 10, New Zealand

Penguin Books Ltd, Registered Offices: Harmondsworth, Middlesex, England

First published 1992
10 9 8 7 6 5 4 3 2 1

Copyright © Peter Hollindale, 1992
All rights reserved

The moral right of the author has been asserted

Filmset in 9/11 pt Monophoto Times
Printed in England by Clays Ltd, St Ives plc

Contents

Critical Studies: A Midsummer Night's Dream

Introductory Note

This study of *A Midsummer Night's Dream* is intended for students who are studying the play in senior forms at school and in universities and colleges. I have assumed that readers will have available a full single-text edition of the play to use alongside this book, and have tried as a matter of policy to omit or condense factual material which any good edition can be trusted to include. Brief advice on the choice of an edition is given in the 'Further Reading' section.

Of all the topics usually treated in editorial matter and critical discussions, the one for which I have been most tempted to find space is a descriptive review of the play's stage history and of recent productions. The life of a play is in the theatre, not in the printed text. However, material of this kind is easily found, and I did not feel that yet another short conducted tour of a critic's theatre-going would add very much to what is freely available already. As a reader I have always found it tantalizing rather than informative to read succinct accounts of productions which I would never have the chance to see. To be really helpful, such production-based critique needs to be extensive and systematic, as it is, for example, in Roger Warren's *A Midsummer Night's Dream: Text and Performance*, a book which interested readers may find complementary to this one. Instead of describing representative productions in a separate section, I have tried in this study to let the play's theatrical life invade the whole discussion. *Everything* about *A Midsummer Night's Dream* – all that comes under the subsidiary headings of 'structure', 'character', 'imagery' or 'theme' – achieves expression in the theatre, and in discussing these topics I have repeatedly sought to unify them as contributory elements in the living wholeness of the play. *A Midsummer Night's Dream*, as I shall try to show, is a complex and intricate play of ideas, but if this discussion works as I hope it may, the reader will be continually aware that these ideas have their life in the sound of voices and the dance of movement on the stage.

The study is designed to close in gradually on the detailed experience of the play. Chapter 1 provides a framework, relating *A Midsummer Night's Dream* to other plays by Shakespeare and to some of his sources in the work of other writers. Chapter 2 provides an overview of the play, relating its plot, ideas and dramatic practice to the overriding subject of marriage and the likely occasion of the play's first performance. In

Chapters 3–6 particular aspects of the play's dramatic practice are examined in much greater detail. The categories here – 'structure', 'character', 'imagery' – are the familiar and conventional ones, but their active presence in *A Midsummer Night's Dream* is unique and unconventional, and in these chapters I have tried to suggest what sets this extraordinary play apart from others. The discussion in these chapters refers mainly to Acts I–IV. Finally, in Chapter 7, the strands of the discussion are drawn together in a detailed consideration of Act V.

Studying a dramatic text is necessarily a very different activity from encountering it in the theatre, and no critical study can hope to mirror the theatrical experience. In this book I have at least tried to show how study of a play's text derives its value from theatrical forms of truth, and to suggest a continuous relationship between reading and seeing, script and performance.

1. Contexts

No Shakespeare play should be studied as an isolated work, but at the theatre this is largely how we experience it; we become wholly involved with the particular event, and are not constantly making comparisons with the rest of Shakespeare's work or detecting borrowings on the dramatist's part from other plays, stories or historical events. Much criticism reflects the audience's standpoint and attends chiefly to the individual play. That is the approach adopted in this study, which is mainly concerned with *A Midsummer Night's Dream* as a single text: its origins, themes and subjects, and dramatic practice. This is a unique play, and the purpose of this book is above all to suggest where that uniqueness lies. In doing this, however, we cannot avoid making comparative references to other plays and groups of plays, to dramatic approaches which have equivalents elsewhere, to characters and stories which were drawn from other works and which the play's first audiences probably knew. Sometimes, indeed, the play expects and depends upon such prior knowledge, employing it for intentional comic and dramatic effects.

Contextual information of this kind, which no longer forms part of the common stock of our minds, needs nowadays to be deliberately brought to our attention. There are two particular kinds of knowledge which can help our understanding of *A Midsummer Night's Dream*: first, the sources from which Shakespeare drew the events, ideas and characters of his play; and second, the other Shakespeare plays which have a close relationship with this one, in genre, theme or date of composition, or some other interesting and potentially helpful way.

Information of these kinds is invariably included in the editorial apparatus of any good edition of the play. To review it comprehensively is a lengthy business, and there is neither space nor need in a study of this kind to summarize or reproduce what is so readily available elsewhere. All students of *A Midsummer Night's Dream* are well advised to obtain an edition of the play which includes a full apparatus; the best ones currently available are listed in the bibliography. When editions consider the play's sources and its companion plays, they rightly seek to be comprehensive and to overlook nothing that we know of or can plausibly guess about the sources Shakespeare drew from.

In this study, concerned as it is with the play's uniqueness, there is a case for selective emphasis on those matters, literary and non-literary, which seem likely to have exercised a special influence on the dramatist, and provided him with refined rather than raw material. These are the subject of the first part of this chapter. The second section is then devoted to a brief review of the other kind of context, the plays which in some way 'belong' with *A Midsummer Night's Dream* and may throw some light on it.

Sources and influences

In the Introduction to the Arden edition of *A Midsummer Night's Dream* Harold F. Brooks quotes approvingly the words of another Shakespeare editor, who argued that literary sources 'are, rightly speaking, the whole relevant contents of the writer's mind as he composes, and no account of them can be complete'. This is well said, and it applies with particular relevance to this play, for two reasons. First, the *Dream* is one of only three Shakespeare plays (the others are *Love's Labour's Lost* and *The Tempest*) where no one has been able to establish the existence of a single dominant source-text. Considered simply as stories, these plays seem to be 'original' compositions in a sense that the other plays are not. Originality, however, is not a matter of inspired and rootless newness, but rather of a freshly created patterning and order composed from what the mind already knows. Second, although we can point to a number of authors, translations and texts from which Shakespeare took part of his material, equally important is a whole range of non-literary sources taken from popular experience, culture and tradition.

Topical events played their part, most notably the bad, unseasonable weather of 1594 which contributed circumstantial detail for Titania's great 'weathers' speech (II.i.81–117). Characteristically of the play, however, this speech owes quite as much to Ovid as it does to meteorological disgruntlement. The play's courtly background is important too, for reasons that are obvious in view of its likely first production (discussed in Chapter 2). Most famous are Oberon's description of the 'mermaid on a dolphin's back' (II.i.150) and the tribute to Queen Elizabeth as the 'imperial votaress' (II.i.163), both of which are traceable to such lavish courtly entertainments as those provided for the Queen at Kenilworth (1591) and Elvetham (1595), where there were fireworks and elaborate water pageants. In courtly pageants of this kind the events which were represented were frequently drawn from Ovid, so that literary sources and famous court occasions conspired to provide a background in Elizabethan culture for

Shakespeare's poetic blend of regality, festival and magic. Popular tradition gave him the fairies, but those we meet in the *Dream* are by no means raw recruits from country superstitions; they derive also from literary sources and courtly romance. Oberon in particular is the product of a mingled ancestry. Chief perhaps amongst them is the romance *Huon of Bordeaux*, in which he is three feet tall, the fairy ruler of a wood where travellers are waylaid and lost. Where the *Dream* has its deepest roots in 'mere England' is not so much in superstitions about fairies (for even the native Robin Goodfellow is considerably revised in the person of Puck), but in the mummers' plays, May games and festive traditions which lie behind the play's excursions to the wood. Such customs were particularly appropriate for use in this play, being both popular and courtly. Their shaping prevalence in the play has been amply demonstrated in C. L. Barber's classic chapter 'May Games and Metamorphoses on a Midsummer Night' in his book *Shakespeare's Festive Comedy*. (This is indispensable reading and, although I propose to quote one extract as a particularly illuminating comment on the working of the play, it is not possible to summarize the chapter effectively; one can only advise students of *A Midsummer Night's Dream* to obtain and read it, for it is one of the landmarks of modern criticism.)

As so many diverse elements come into view, these observations on the play by the eminent folklorist Dr Katharine Briggs seem entirely apt:

The more one ponders over *A Midsummer Night's Dream* the more remarkable it appears. All sources are drawn on for the material of the play, but the result is a shining unity. Theseus and Hippolyta, half classical, half medieval, hunt through the wood; the lovers, romantic after Chaucer's tradition, but a little perhaps forgetting Chaucer's manners, quarrel in it; the Elizabethan tradesmen rehearse in it; a league away at Athens Diana's votaresses are chanting hymns to the moon; but the wood is in Warwickshire, with its brakes of sweet brier and beds of primroses and banks of wild thyme. In the same way Oberon derives through Huon of Bordeaux from Alberich, the German dwarf, Titania inherits the rites of Diana, by the late classical tradition of the gods descended into fairies, the Celtic Pouk shares a character with English Robin Goodfellow, and shows the traits of the Boggy Beast, the Brag and the Grant; yet the fairies, like Queen Elizabeth, are 'mere English'.

(*The Anatomy of Puck*, p. 44)

The play in fact is an astonishing act of eclecticism. It gathers into itself a large and disparate set of contributory influences, and creates from them a unity which is not just the result of deft and successful grafting, or even integration, but something newly created and original.

In relation to the fairies and to Puck, the process of eclectic creativity is admirably set out by C. L. Barber:

As a matter of fact there is much less popular lore in these fairies than is generally assumed in talking about them. The fairies do, it is true, show all the main characteristics of fairies in popular belief: they appear in the forest, at midnight, and leave at sunrise; they take children, dance in ringlets. But . . . their whole quality is drastically different from that of the fairies 'of the villagery', creatures who . . . were dangerous to meddle with, large enough to harm, often malicious . . . one can look at what [Shakespeare] did in relation to the traditions of holiday and pageantry and see his creatures as pageant nymphs and holiday celebrants, coloured by touches from popular superstition, but shaped primarily by a very different provenance. Most of the detailed popular lore concerns Puck, not properly a fairy at all; even he is several parts Cupid and several parts mischievous stage page (a cousin of Moth in *Love's Labour's Lost* and no doubt played by the same small, agile boy).

(*Shakespeare's Festive Comedy*, p. 144)

This mischievous, Cupid-like boy accords, as I shall mention later, with the most convincing way I have seen the part played. But the Celtic Pouk, referred to by Katharine Briggs, was not boyish or Cupid-like at all, nor did he have anything in common with the classical Mercury or Hermes, the messenger of the gods, who also seems to be present in the role. As Dr Minor White Latham reminds us in her study of *The Elizabethan Fairies*, 'the term *Puck* or *pouke* was a generic term applied to a class of demons or devils and the devil himself', and he was a large figure, at least the size of a fully grown man, both tall and thickset. From such diverse progenitors Shakespeare fashioned his own captivating, impudent and stealthy spirit.

Likewise Titania is at once the blending of contributory presences and a wholly fresh creation who is unlike them all. 'Titania' is a name in Ovid for Diana (*Metamorphoses*, III), which helps to explain her sometimes incongruous identification with chastity, and her authority over an order of female votaresses practising their celibate idyll on the Indian seashore. But she is also in another part of her being the May queen of popular custom, and it is partly in that residual role as a fertility goddess that she makes her entry into Theseus' court, just as her real-life equivalents might have done to the great country houses of Elizabethan England. In the pageant at Elvetham, as Brooks notes, 'a dancing round of fairies was led by their queen, who named herself Auberon's consort'. Yet another of her derivations was from Proserpina, wife of 'Pluto that is kyng of Fayerye', in Chaucer's *Merchant's Tale*. This pair of watchful deities make merry, in the manner of the reconciled Oberon and Titania, whenever they happen to be on good terms with one another:

> Ful often tyme he Pluto and his queene
> Proserpina, and al hire fayerye,
> Disporten hem and maken melodye
> About that welle, and daunced, as men tolde
> *(The Merchant's Tale*, 2038–41)

But the pair are also quarrelsome, like Oberon and Titania, disputing bitterly with each other about the respective merits of male and female, and exercising benevolent but jealous patronage over fallible human lovers.

Despite her composite ancestry, however, Shakespeare's Titania is wholly individualized. Even her momentary incongruities are harmonized by comedy and form complementary aspects of her formidable power. Such diverse associations as all these make up a unified original.

A similar blending, unifying process is observable in Shakespeare's indebtedness to his individual source-texts in themselves, where it is sometimes possible to trace seemingly unconnected contributions to the *Dream* which yet form an eventual part of the play's unity and uniqueness. One classic source for Bottom's transformation is in Lucius Apuleius, *The Transformations of Lucius*, better known as *The Golden Ass*. Several episodes of this bawdy masterpiece seem to have contributed to *A Midsummer Night's Dream*. Lucius, transformed into an ass, has the belated good fortune to be adopted into the household of a nobleman called Thyasus, who is much diverted by his ability to perform human tricks, and treats him with kindness. As the ass becomes famous and attracts visitors, he earns the seductive attentions of a rich noblewoman. Their subsequent lovemaking and its complications are racily translated by Robert Graves: 'All the same, I was worried, very worried indeed, at the thought of sleeping with so lovely a woman: my great hairy legs and hard hoofs pressed against her milk-and-honey skin – her dewy red lips kissed by my huge mouth with its ugly great teeth.' This unseemly carnal farce seems to provide a clear precedent for the more decorous amours of Titania and Bottom. Elsewhere in the work, too, is the inset story of Cupid and Psyche. Cupid becomes Psyche's lover, but their meeting comes about because Cupid is fulfilling the spiteful commission of his mother, Venus, to punish Psyche for her charms: his orders are to make Psyche fall in love with some low, unworthy object.

If these echoes connect *The Golden Ass* with the amorous parts of Bottom's adventure, the transformation of Lucius back to his own shape suggests its visionary aftermath. Lucius prays to the goddess Isis, begging to be restored to his human form, and, as a sign that his prayer is granted, he is shown a vision of the goddess herself:

> I returned to my sandy hollow, where once more sleep overcame me. I had scarcely closed my eyes before the apparition of a woman began to rise from the middle of the sea ... I will try to describe this transcendent vision, for though human speech is poor and limited, the Goddess herself will perhaps inspire me ...

(*The Golden Ass*, trans. Robert Graves, p. 227)

Although this is not the only source of Bottom's wonderful experiences, and although Shakespeare once again made something quite original from what he used, there is clear evidence here of loosely related debts to a particular text. What Shakespeare made of them illustrates very well the process of imaginative fusion which produced *A Midsummer Night's Dream*. It also confirms the special interest and imaginative importance for Shakespeare of transformations, and in particular the continuum from comic sexual grotesquerie to dreamlike and transfiguring vision.

If there is a major source-text for *A Midsummer Night's Dream*, it must be Ovid's *Metamorphoses*, in the 1567 translation by Arthur Golding with which Shakespeare was familiar. Ovid's work suggested a number of particular references, one example of which we have noted in the case of Titania's 'weathers' speech. Because Ovid's work was widely known to educated Elizabethans, and drawn upon for the narrative materials of festive pageantry, it also provided Shakespeare with a form of cultural currency which was shared with his audience, and therefore allowed him scope for economical and surreptitious humour as well as melodramatic suggestiveness. Above all, it supplied the major classical precedent for the theme of metamorphosis or transformation which lies at the very heart of *A Midsummer Night's Dream*. Here is an example, then, of a multiply influential source text affecting the dramatist at every level, from unifying thematic generality to minor elements of plotting.

The most conspicuous single contribution made by Ovid is the story of Pyramus and Thisbe (Book IV of *Metamorphoses*). Translator as well as poet played their part in Peter Quince's interlude, as is evident in this short extract from Golding's translation:

The wall that parted house from house had riven therein a crany
Which shronke at making of the wall. This fault not markt of any
Of many hundred yeares before (what doth not love espie?)
These lovers first of all found out, and made a way whereby
To talk together secretly . . .

(*Metamorphoses*, IV, 83–7)

In Golding's version, as in other translations that Shakespeare probably knew, the story of Pyramus and Thisbe is largely ridiculous. Farce and tragedy are intermingled in the story itself, which has ready potential for 'tragical mirth' and 'hot ice'. The inherent risk of mortifying laughter is much increased by the oddities and stylistic ineptitudes of the English versions in themselves. Shakespeare would have had no difficulty from his reading of Golding alone in seeing the dramatic possibilities for such a farcical production as Peter Quince's. On the other hand, behind the absurdities he could also see the truth of a potentially catastrophic love affair brought to disaster by parental opposition and obstruction. Indeed he had chosen just this theme for treatment as a tragedy in *Romeo and Juliet*, the nearest play to *A Midsummer Night's Dream* in date of composition, and probably written immediately before it. Here, therefore, are all the circumstances to hand for the uniquely effective placement of 'Pyramus and Thisbe' within the design of *A Midsummer Night's Dream*: a farcical representation of tragic events, both hilarious in itself and reflecting back with ironic effect on the earlier ordeal of the lovers. Contained in the use of 'Pyramus and Thisbe' is the opportunity for comic parallel with the antics of the four lovers, whose experiences are farcical in a different way, who themselves negotiate a brush with possible disaster, whose comic trials are also caused by parental tyranny, and who can be brought safe and sound into the on-stage audience for the mechanicals' play. It is from his sources, therefore, that Shakespeare took his cue for a double effect of tragedy covered with farce.

Amongst the versions of the story that he knew there is one which is *not* ridiculous, and this too may have been instrumental in suggesting the effects he could achieve. The exception is Chaucer's version of the story in *The Legend of Good Women*. As Pyramus and Thisbe in this version plot their elopement, the different tone of Chaucer's lines may have helped to suggest the parallel with the escape from Athens of Lysander and Hermia, and hence an event where comedy of circumstances does not cancel out the reality of love:

> Unto this clyft, as it was wont to be,
> Com Piramus, and after com Thysbe,
> And plyghten trouthe fully in here fey
> That ilke same nyght to stele awey,
> And to begile here wardeyns everichon,
> And forth out of the cite for to goon;
> And, for the feldes ben so brode and wide,
> For to mete in o place at o tyde . . .
>   (*The Legend of Good Women,* 776–83)

Once again, then, the intricate, unified and original dramatic experience of *A Midsummer Night's Dream* is traceable (even if speculatively) to diverse material in the available sources.

Another work by Chaucer is an indisputable source-text for *A Midsummer Night's Dream,* and it too is used in several different ways; this is *The Knight's Tale.* Chaucer's tale, like Shakespeare's play, opens with Theseus' conquest of, and marriage to, Hippolyta, and (as in Shakespeare) this provides a 'framing' situation of mature, established love which surrounds the passions and the trials of younger and more accident-prone lovers. The newly-married Theseus, acting in chivalrous response to the pleas of grieving women, wages war on Creon, ruler of Thebes. Victorious, Theseus takes prisoner two young knights, Palamon and Arcite, who during their captivity espy and fall in love with Emelye, Hippolyta's sister. The rivalry which then develops between them has several parallels with *A Midsummer Night's Dream.* Palamon and Arcite, like Lysander and Demetrius, are almost indistinguishable in character – but not quite. Each of them solicits the favour of a patron deity – Palamon sacrifices to Venus, goddess of love, and Arcite to Mars, god of war – and such minor differences as we can find between them are attributable to words and behaviour appropriate to their chosen benefactor. Equivalent slight differences between Demetrius and Lysander might plausibly be explained by a differential balance between aggression and romance. After much suffering for love, Palamon and Arcite meet each other in a wood near Athens. Instead of being frustrated in attempts to fight, as Lysander and Demetrius are, they fight a duel with each other. They are discovered and interrupted by Theseus, who (like Shakespeare's Theseus) is out hunting with his hounds and horn on a May morning. Though Chaucer's Theseus is more severe than Shakespeare's, he too is just, thoughtful, rational and wise, and, after recovering from initial anger, he arranges for the rivalry of Palamon and Arcite to be settled in a tournament. Since in Chaucer's tale there is only one woman, there can be only one victor and one marriage, so there is no such scope as there is in *A Midsummer Night's Dream* for a uniformly happy ending. However, the way the dilemma is resolved has interesting implications for our reading of Shakespeare's play.

The Knight's Tale, like *A Midsummer Night's Dream*, is much concerned with balance and symmetry. As in Shakespeare, there is symmetry of characters, locales, events, ideas and narrative structures. In both works we have a sense of poise and elegance of intellect as well as imaginative energy. The resolution of the conflict in Chaucer's tale reflects this balance. Arcite, the client of Mars, is granted victory in the tournament: he 'wins the war' and so wins Emelye. The pride of Mars is satisfied. Before he can marry her, however, he is thrown from his horse by the gods' contrivance and dies of his injuries. The surviving Palamon, client of Venus, is then granted Emelye's hand; he wins the love and the lady. The pride of Venus is satisfied. The tale concludes with a long philosophical discourse by Theseus, justifying the workings of providence by means of stoic rationality.

Chaucer's Theseus is wise, intelligent, rational and wrong. We the readers know, as Theseus does not, that the contest between Palamon and Arcite has been decided by a rancorous squabble upstairs among the gods, and that Venus and Mars have been concerned not with rational justice but with their own pride. The symmetry of technically ordered justice – Arcite wins the fight, Palamon wins Emelye – is not justice at all, but a ruthless trick of opportunistic face-saving devised by cunning old Saturn. Its purpose is to ensure that no divine nose is out of joint. There are more and nastier things in heaven than Theseus' orderly philosophy takes account of.

It is not, I think, too fanciful to see what riches lay in *The Knight's Tale* for Shakespeare to seize upon. Some of the *Dream*'s debts to *The Knight's Tale* are beyond dispute. More speculatively, one can see in Chaucer's tale a model of interactive content and form, of symmetrical organization, which Shakespeare was able to use and replicate for his own, very different, purposes. More speculatively still, but in my view convincingly, one can see in Chaucer's Theseus a model of the aspirations and the limits of human reason, its heroic and necessary, but ultimately doomed, attempts to place a rational enclosure round the vast and mysterious periphery of existence. In Chaucer the things beyond human knowledge and reason are threatening, taking the form of selfish, petty and ruthless gods. In Shakespeare too they are occasionally threatening, taking the form of angry elements, discordant natural forces, churchyard sprites. Dominant in *A Midsummer Night's Dream*, however, are 'spirits of another sort', made from the realities of imagination, dream and vision, 'more than cool reason ever comprehends'. Because Theseus is admirable, reason is not traduced, but because (like Chaucer's Theseus) he 'comprehends' less than we do, the imagination is emancipated.

The Shakespearean context

A Midsummer Night's Dream is a particularly difficult play to fit into the usual subcategories of Shakespeare criticism. The comedies are commonly separated for convenience into two main groups: the 'early comedies' which include *The Comedy of Errors*, *The Taming of the Shrew* and *The Two Gentlemen of Verona*, and the 'mature comedies' which include *As You Like It*, *Twelfth Night* and *Much Ado About Nothing*. There is also a further group of plays written at the end of Shakespeare's career, sometimes called 'romances' or simply 'late plays', but sometimes 'late comedies'; they include *The Winter's Tale* and *The Tempest*. *A Midsummer Night's Dream*, which is itself an early play, has features in common with at least one play from each of these three groups, although its closest neighbour among the comedies (in date as well as form) is *Love's Labour's Lost*, another play which cannot easily be categorized as 'early' or 'mature'. To complicate things still further, there are several respects in which the *Dream*'s closest Shakespearean relative is not a comedy at all, but the tragedy *Romeo and Juliet*. Perhaps this is a sign that we should give more readily to the comedies the same flexibility of approach and regard for the single unique play that we habitually bring to the tragedies.

Leaving aside for a moment *Love's Labour's Lost*, the work of early Shakespeare comedy which most closely anticipates *A Midsummer Night's Dream* is *The Two Gentlemen of Verona*. This, too, is the story of four lovers, initially balanced and symmetrical but then disrupted because one of the male lovers changes his allegiance. Proteus falls in love with Julia, and Valentine with Silvia. The two men are close friends, both natives of Verona, both sent to Milan to further their courtly education. Julia lives in Verona, Silvia in Milan. The balanced love quartet is completed when the unattached Valentine is sent to Milan and there falls in love with Silvia, but disrupted when Proteus is forcibly made to follow him, leaving Julia behind. Arrived in Milan, he too falls in love with Silvia, is therefore false to Julia, and betrays his friend. Since the love of Valentine and Silvia is already secret, conducted in defiance of Silvia's Egeus-like and tyrannous father, the two lovers are separated, and Valentine is exiled to the forest, where he adopts a strange career of courtly banditry. Matters are finally resolved when all the lovers, along with the despotic father, are brought together in the melting-pot of the forest, and true faithful loves are re-formed and accepted. The lovers are joined, the friendship of Proteus and Valentine is renewed, the father reconciled, and the ridiculous plot concluded.

Several features of *A Midsummer Night's Dream* are apparent: the symmetry of the love quartet, disrupted by sudden treachery of passion, the betrayal of friendship, the tyrannous parent, the transformative forest. It is not *Two Gentlemen*'s plot as a whole which is ridiculous (it observes the conventions and generates the complications proper to comedy) but the final scene, into which is crammed a hectic series of implausible psychological conversions. The pace of events, together with an insufficient gap between realism and convention, turn everything to absurdity. What the comparison reveals is that fairy magic makes the love conversions of *A Midsummer Night's Dream* not less but more believable, setting the irrational abruptness of love's volatility within a framework of supportive fantasy. Paradoxically, the influential presence of supernatural magic makes our play a more persuasive dramatization of human love.

Love's Labour's Lost, in contrast with *The Two Gentlemen of Verona*, is a brilliant and sophisticated courtly comedy in which artifice is all-important. The King of Navarre and three of his attendant lords determine upon a self-imposed discipline of celibacy, spartan life and study which will last three years. No sooner have they committed themselves by oath to this ambitious lunacy than their plans are interrupted by the arrival of the Princess of France, entrusted with a diplomatic mission and accompanied by three attendant ladies. This convenient sexual symmetry has predictable consequences. The play does not enact unfaithfulness in love, only unfaithfulness to idiotic vows of abstention.

Compared with *A Midsummer Night's Dream*, *Love's Labour's Lost* is a witty, urbane and cerebral play, with little of the *Dream*'s liberating enhancement of poetic vision. Despite this, it is recognizably the work of the same dramatist at the same period. It is like the *Dream* in its symmetrical plotting. This extends even to a qualified happy ending in which all the ladies delay their consent to marriage and impose an intervening year of harsh and punitive atonement to set against the self-indulgent hairshirt ordeal that the courtiers first intended. There are resemblances of setting too. Because Navarre and his friends have barred their house to ladies, the whole significant action takes place in the king's park, a suitably elegant pastoral equivalent of the Athenian groves. Most obvious and important, though, is the two plays' similarity of structure. Each has a programme of entangled love ending with a fifth-act promise of harmony, and each has a last-act 'play-within-a-play' comprising inept theatrical entertainment, provided in *Love's Labour's Lost* by yokels, locals and courtly hangers-on. Appropriately to the sophisticated, cutting brilliancy of *Love's Labour's Lost*, this equivalent episode is far crueller on the part of the on-stage audience than anything which Bottom and company undergo, but the difference in effect is derived from major structural resemblance.

Of the recognized 'mature comedies', it is *As You Like It* which most closely matches *A Midsummer Night's Dream.* In this play, too, an inhospitable courtly environment (far more perilous than Theseus' Athens) is deserted for a greenwood refuge, the forest of Arden. In *As You Like It* there are neither rivalries nor infidelities of love, but rather the comedy of enforced concealment, of courtship and of love's confession. The complications of the plot are such that a troubled departure from the court is eventually reversed by a happy return. A set of marriages and a masque of Hymen conclude this play's version of a displaced environment which permits transformative love. The parallel should not be pursued too far. Except for the masque itself there is no magic in *As You Like It*, and no penumbra of surrounding mystery such as that which gives *A Midsummer Night's Dream* its unique form of imaginative release. Even so there are continuities of interest and dramatic practice. The pattern of excursion and return, of court to country and back again, is essentially the same; so is the comic parallelism between very different kinds of love; so is the enactment of blatantly incongruous love which throws into happy relief the true and permanent achieved relationships; so is the closing celebratory performance of spectacle, blessing and dance; so is the close thematic intertwining of love and courtesy; so is the containing preoccupation with benevolent and civilized rule. It is also worth noting that Arden, like the Athenian grove, is a dual-natured setting: it is on the one hand pastoral and innocent, a place for idealized shepherds, just as the fairy kingdom is rich with flowers and water, but on the other hand it is a dangerous place where wild beasts roam and solitary travellers are endangered. There are snakes in both forests.

The Tempest is a very late play, a 'romance', separated by many years from *A Midsummer Night's Dream* in date of composition and in many respects a very different kind of play; yet it is probably true that *A Midsummer Night's Dream*, more than any other play of Shakespeare's earlier maturity, foreshadows that concluding dramatic vision. Love and marriage are ancillary rather than central preoccupations in *The Tempest*, but they are the essential agents of reconciliation and renewal for imperfect and inconstant humankind. Arbitrary eruptions of faithlessness and treachery are not confined to youthful love and courtship in the late plays; indeed, youthful love is finally presented as a dependable and redeeming constancy amongst surrounding imperfections. In a sense, the order of dependable security is reversed; it is the lovers who in the late plays are the still centre of a turning world.

Magic, however, is common to the two plays. In *The Tempest*, as in *A Midsummer Night's Dream*, we are in an imaginative world which admits the form of things unknown. Oberon is the prime custodian of magic in *A Midsummer Night's Dream*, and in this study I argue for his power as an essential complement to that of Theseus; the world of night complements the world of day, magic and imagination complement and enhance reason. In *The Tempest* the presiding figure of Prospero is both Theseus and Oberon in one being; the daylight philosopher of sane morality is also the magician and commander of the spirits. Among the spirits attendant upon Prospero, Ariel is the closest relative in all Shakespeare to the figure of Puck. They share the physicality of graceful swiftness; they share an independence of being which observes and yet transcends mere service; they have a markedly different yet corresponding blend of impish, delighted mischief and protective benevolence. Ariel could say with Puck, 'Lord, what fools these mortals be.' Being 'kindlier moved' than Puck, he doesn't, but he is just as good at leading them astray, through bush and brier.

Indications such as these allow us to note the deeper connections of interest between the two plays: the balance between nature and art, the magical inducement of transformation which is in harmony with natural processes of time and growth and change, and the significance of sleep and dream.

In 1613, at the very end of his career, Shakespeare collaborated with John Fletcher on a play which in some features of plot and theme bears the closest resemblance to *A Midsummer Night's Dream* of all the plays. This is the rarely performed *The Two Noble Kinsmen*, which was not included in the First Folio of Shakespeare's plays (1623) and is still occasionally omitted from editions of his collected works. Despite this, Shakespeare's hand in its composition, especially in the first and last acts, is beyond serious dispute.

Some strong resemblances are not surprising, because *The Two Noble Kinsmen* is a dramatization of Chaucer's *The Knight's Tale*, which as we have seen already was one of Shakespeare's major sources for the

Dream. Hence Theseus is once again the 'framing' figure of authority and justice. In this role he is (appropriately to *The Knight's Tale*) a more severe figure than the Theseus of our early comedy, but he has the same essentially benevolent desire for orderly justice. Like Chaucer's Theseus, and like the Duke of *A Midsummer Night's Dream* as the intellectual devotee of reason, the Theseus of *The Two Noble Kinsmen* is a would-be philosopher-king. He tries but is finally unable to bring the caprices of human fate within the bounds of rational intelligence and understanding. However, there are many differences which clearly place *The Two Noble Kinsmen* among the late plays. Theseus' efforts to interpret the irrationalities of human experience are here more perfunctory and less strenuous than those of either of his namesakes in *The Knight's Tale* and the *Dream*, but they are also arguably more successful because marked by the final acceptance and serenity which distinguish the late romances.

Other features of the plot are common ground between *A Midsummer Night's Dream* and *The Two Noble Kinsmen*. Both plays open with preparations for the marriage of Theseus and Hippolyta, establishing their mature relationship as a framing device for the volatile rivalries of young love. Like *A Midsummer Night's Dream* and *Love's Labour's Lost*, *The Two Noble Kinsmen* has a play-within-a-play made up of an over-ambitious theatrical performance by amateurs for a courtly audience, although in this play it occurs in the middle rather than at the end. In both *A Midsummer Night's Dream* and *The Two Noble Kinsmen*, a nocturnal conflict between rival lovers is discovered by Theseus in the course of a May morning hunting party. Some, but not all, of these similarities of plot can be ascribed to the sharing of a common Chaucerian source.

A particularly interesting feature of *The Two Noble Kinsmen* is a dialogue between Emilia and Hippolyta about a girlhood friendship amounting virtually to twinning of identity (*The Two Noble Kinsmen*, I.iii.48–85), which is almost a replica in thought and feeling of Helena's commemoration of her childhood union with Hermia (*A Midsummer Night's Dream*, III.ii.195–219). Such late evidence of Shakespeare's continuing interest in this interlinked pattern of structure, scenes, ideas and themes can serve to illustrate the lasting achievement of *A Midsummer Night's Dream*. It may be an 'early' comedy, but in no way is it an immature one.

Romeo and Juliet is ostensibly the strangest, and yet in some respects the closest, companion-piece for *A Midsummer Night's Dream*. It was probably written slightly earlier, and the relationship between the two

plays lies in similarities of theme, resemblances of style and verbal echoes which suggest the familiarity in Shakespeare's mind of the first play as he composed the second. Sometimes there is a discernible reflection through comedy, as if at least a part of Shakespeare's recall had led him to amused self-parody. Certainly there are marked correspondences of situation between *Romeo and Juliet* and 'Pyramus and Thisbe'. In both dramatic works a pair of star-crossed lovers seek a clandestine fulfilment in the face of parental hostility. In *Romeo and Juliet* it is the antagonism between the houses of Montague and Capulet by which Romeo and Juliet are defeated when they fall in love. A fateful error of circumstance precipitates the tragic finale, when Romeo finds Juliet dead, as he thinks, though in reality she is in a drugged sleep. Romeo commits suicide. Juliet then awakes from her deathlike coma and finds his body, whereupon she too commits suicide, stabbing herself. If *Romeo and Juliet* is indeed the slightly earlier play, as seems likely, then Shakespeare cannot have been unaware of the incongruous plot-resemblance he was perpetrating. The dating of the two plays, as well as the conscious reminiscence, is confirmed by the Nurse's lines in *Romeo and Juliet*, when Juliet's 'body' is discovered and, according to plan, mistakenly believed to be a corpse:

> O woe! O woeful, woeful, woeful day!
> Most lamentable day, most woeful day
> That ever, ever I did yet behold!
> O day, O day, O day! O hateful day!
> Never was seen so black a day as this.
> O woeful day! O woeful day!
> (*Romeo and Juliet*, IV.v.49–54)

Even granted that the nurse is a comic character, it is hard to believe that Shakespeare could have put such words in his foremost tragedy of youth if he had already written 'Pyramus and Thisbe', or conversely that certain of Bottom's lines as Pyramus were not an amused reflection on his own stylistic excess.

Primarily, however, the plays exchange imaginative respect. Lysander's lament for the obstacles and tragedies of love in Act I of *A Midsummer Night's Dream* not only bears generally on several of the circumstances which destroy Romeo and Juliet, but closely echoes the tragedy. Lysander's vision of love, 'Brief as the lightning in the collied night', is imaginatively at one with Juliet's fears for her new love:

> I have no joy of this contract tonight.
> It is too rash, too unadvised, too sudden;
> Too like the lightning, which doth cease to be
> Ere one can say 'It lightens'.
> > (*Romeo and Juliet*, II.ii.117–20)

Romeo and Juliet is, so to speak, the dark underside of *A Midsummer Night's Dream*, its counterpart in lyrical tragedy and the disastrous fulfilment of those alternative fates for youthful love which are glancingly suggested in the comedy. They are avoided in the action of the *Dream* by good fortune and beneficent interventions, and finally set at comic distance by the mechanicals' play. Avoided though they are, they are not denied existence in the comedy. The imaginative conception of the two plays in fact has much in common. They show the analysis of love and its duality of strangeness and truth. *Romeo and Juliet* begins with just such an instance of love's fickleness and sudden arbitrary change as affects the lovers in the *Dream*, when Romeo on the instant drops his infatuation with one Rosaline as soon as he catches sight of Juliet. The beginning of the tragedy might just as well in some ways be the beginning of a comedy, and especially *this* comedy. The preoccupation with differences between doting and loving, with the functions of the eye, with sweetness turning to loathsomeness, is shared by the two plays.

Above all, however, there is the overriding contrast between day and night, light and dark, sun and moon, which brings the two works into close imaginative accord. Their emphases and effects are different. *Romeo and Juliet* is full of daylight consciousness, and hot sunlight is as much its zone of social danger in the streets of Verona as the darkness is its zone of vulnerable private love. But the interpenetrative image of light and dark is essentially the same, and the darkness has its same corollary of dreaming. In Romeo's words to Juliet we are a very short distance indeed from the vision of *A Midsummer Night's Dream*:

> O blessèd, blessèd night! I am afeard,
> Being in night, all this is but a dream,
> Too flattering-sweet to be substantial.
> > (*Romeo and Juliet*, II.ii.139–141)

The two plays are doing very different things, and taking even their common imagery in very different directions, but recognizably from the same base-camp of imagination.

2. The Marriage Play

The courtly origins

In John Caird's 1989 production of *A Midsummer Night's Dream* for the Royal Shakespeare Company both Puck and the fairies were played as children. Puck, dressed in schoolboy grey shorts and tie, and latterly with a school cap also, was a mischievous and clever juvenile prankster. It was a witty and iconoclastic version of the role, and Shakespeare's practical joker lost little of his characteristic nature by acquiring some extra touches from *Just William*. The fairies too were dressed and played as if they were child actors, performing with some evident embarrassment in parts they had outgrown. Ungainly mixtures of tutu and black boots, along with spotty and unprettied faces, deliberately robbed them of the airy and ethereal beauty which so many generations of romantic staging have struggled to convey. The costuming of this production was one episode in the determined demystification of *A Midsummer Night's Dream* which has figured largely in its recent theatrical history. Instead of fairyland and fluid, balletic movement, the director had found in these scenes the pretext for a comic gawky childishness.

This way of playing Puck was a success, the fairies less so, and this would not have surprised the critic Ernest Schanzer who distinguished between three 'wholly distinct kinds of fairies' in the play, and said of Puck: 'He is the complete opposite of the tiny fairies with whom Shakespeare fills Oberon's and Titania's train, being gross and earthy, boisterous, rough and boyish, where the tiny fairies are aerial, timid and courteous. Nothing could be more misleading than to speak of them as irresponsible children, as so many critics do . . .' (*Casebook*, p. 70).

Yet children of some noble house may once have figured as named or supernumerary fairies in the earliest production of *A Midsummer Night's Dream* if we accept the widespread belief that the play was first performed to grace the wedding feast of some unidentified Elizabethan patron of Shakespeare's company of players, later called the Lord Chamberlain's Men. The number of children required to cast the play may have exceeded those usually available as juvenile professionals within the company, which has strengthened in the minds of some critics the likelihood that the play originates in aristocratic festivities taking place in a noble household. C. L. Barber has suggested that 'It seems quite possible that Peaseblossom, Cobweb, Moth and Mustardseed were originally played by children of the family – their parts seem designed to be foolproof for little children: "Ready! – And I! – And I! – And I!"'. Indeed, Barber opens his discussion with a categorical statement: 'To honour a noble wedding, Shakespeare gathered up in a play the sort of pageantry which was usually presented piecemeal at aristocratic entertainments, in park and court as well as in hall' (*Shakespeare's Festive Comedy*, p. 119). His assumption is shared by, amongst many others, R. W. Dent, who recognizes the absence of external evidence that such an occasion marked the play's first performance, but observes nevertheless that 'the internal evidence that *A Midsummer Night's Dream* was either written or adapted for a courtly wedding seems to me, as to most, overwhelming'.

There is in fact no firm evidence of any kind to link *A Midsummer Night's Dream* with any courtly wedding, except what can be inferred from the text itself. A number of weddings have been suggested as possible occasions for the play's first performance, but the whole matter is speculative and is unlikely ever to be resolved. Any likely claimants to the inaugural production must be compatible with the period during which we know the play was written, and it is generally placed between 1594 and 1596. This rules out a number of suggested contenders. The possibilities are lucidly presented by Harold Brooks in his Introduction to the Arden edition of the play. The marriage of Frances, Lady Sidney to the Earl of Essex in 1590 is much too early, and that of the Earl of Southampton and Elizabeth Vernon in 1598 is much too late. So is the marriage of Henry, Lord Herbert and Anne Russell in 1600. A nearer miss is that of the Countess of Southampton and Sir Thomas Heneage in the spring of 1594, the limits of probable dating ruling out what might otherwise be an intriguing possibility. There remain two other plausible occasions. The first was the wedding of Elizabeth Vere and William, Earl of Derby, which was celebrated at Greenwich, where the court was sitting, on 26 January 1595. This wedding has the attraction of a strong association with the Queen, who is the recipient of a famously graceful compliment in the play. Elizabeth Vere was the granddaughter of Lord Burghley, the most powerful, trusted and successful of Queen Elizabeth's Secretaries of State, and the bride herself was one of the Queen's maids of honour. The Queen was present at the wedding feast which took place at Burghley House in the Strand.

Despite the temptations of this wedding, however, the most persuasive case can be made for the marriage of Elizabeth Carey and Thomas, son of Henry, Lord Berkeley, on 19 February 1596. The date is more convincing, but the strongest argument of all is that this marriage combines evident royal favour (even if the Queen's actual presence is unproven) and a direct link with Shakespeare's company of actors. Elizabeth Carey was one of the Queen's god-daughters. Her grandfather was Henry, Lord Hunsdon, the Queen's Lord Chamberlain, and at the time of this marriage Shakespeare's company enjoyed his patronage as Lord Hunsdon's Men. Her father, Sir George Carey, was high in the Queen's favour, and became the patron of Shakespeare's company after the death of Lord Hunsdon in 1596; when Carey succeeded his father as Lord Chamberlain in 1597, the company became the Lord Chamberlain's Men. The combination of the suitable wedding date, the aristocratic prestige and royal favour of the married couple and the bride's family, and the close family link with the actors, makes this the most convincing claimant to a celebratory first performance of the play.

There are dissenting voices which remain unconvinced that any such private performance is the likely origin of the comedy (pointing out, for example, that such entertainment usually took the form of masques, and that the fashion for them came some years later). Prominent among the sceptics is Stanley Wells, who has cogently restated his doubts in a recent article. He points to new evidence which weakens the claims of the Carey/Berkeley wedding. However, most students of the play continue to believe that this is how it began. But everything is conjecture, nothing is proven fact, and whatever private courtly origins the play may have had, it undeniably made a rapid and successful crossing to the public theatres, where its appeal to popular taste lies in the affirmation that it had soon been 'sundry times publickely acted'.

In the discussion which follows, the main emphasis falls on the thematic prominence of marriage in the play: it is an integral, organic and continuous subject in this drama to an extent unparalleled in any other Shakespeare comedy. However, I have adopted the 'court wedding' hypothesis in order to show that the play's theatrical nature makes it quite exceptionally *appropriate* for such an occasion, and that by imagining such a performance we can extend our understanding of the play itself.

Marital interludes

Whatever its origins, the special status of *A Midsummer Night's Dream* as a 'marriage play' is clear from internal evidence alone. Naturally there is nothing unusual in a comedy's culminating in a set of happy marriages; a similar outcome ends the play which is in most respects the closest parallel to *A Midsummer Night's Dream* in Shakespeare's comic practice and development, *Love's Labour's Lost* (though in that play the felicitous marital consummation is made subject to a disciplinary and purgatorial delay). There are happy marital completions after troubled courtships at the end of all the comedies, a convention of final conjugal harmony which is subsequently brought under sceptical and disturbing critique in the 'problem comedies' or 'anti-comedies', *Measure for Measure* and *All's Well That Ends Well. As You Like It*, the play which competes with *A Midsummer Night's Dream* for status as the happiest of all the 'happy comedies' (to borrow John Dover Wilson's term for the group), ends with a masque of Hymen which gives formal and ritual unification to the mixed assortment of ideal and dubious matches which make up its ending. Even *As You Like It*, however, *arrives* at marriage as the unifying centrepiece of its finale rather than being unbrokenly concerned with it throughout.

A Midsummer Night's Dream, by contrast, is preoccupied with marriage, and with love leading to marriage, from the first scene to the last. All the tribulations of love and courtship which variously dominate its non-Athenian scenes are framed by a place and a time which is given over to secure affiance and imminent marriage celebration. Of all the play's prolific intricacies of symmetrical design, which I shall seek to identify in this study, this is one which provides attractive empirical suggestion that a sophisticated wedding feast was indeed the likely occasion for the play's first performance. The whole play, so to speak, occurs in an interval.

Act I begins with Theseus' instructions to Philostrate that he should 'Stir up the Athenian youth to merriments', and institute a period of festive action which will both duly celebrate the happiness of marriage and occupy the laggard days before the event is consummated in the sexual peace of marital union. (There are four days to be filled in before the wedding day, though in the relaxed, unworried time-scheme of Shakespearean comedy these four days have collapsed into three or even two by the time we reach the ending.) Act V begins with similar employment of Philostrate, required to produce diversionary entertainment for the final slowcoach evening, the three hours' wait before the clock strikes and 'the iron tongue of midnight hath told twelve'. Time's decorum must be ritually observed. Its last phase is filled up by the lamentable comedy of 'Pyramus and Thisbe', a sadly inappropriate tale for a wedding night, made comically appropriate by the wonderful inability of its participants to discriminate successfully between imagination and fact, vision and reality, self and role. The stage audience, having a sophisticated understanding of theatrical truth which the actors lack, enjoys the unintended comedy, and one of the play's last acts of festive mischief is to remind the stage audience that after all their impatience with the slowness of time, they have allowed the mechanicals' thespian endeavours to divert them too successfully, and keep them up too long.

Yet several members of this same stage audience have themselves unknowingly enacted an equivalent entertainment in uncomprehending, unintentional response to the first of Theseus' injunctions to Philostrate. The Athenian youth, in the persons of Lysander, Hermia, Demetrius and Helena, has indeed been 'stirred up to merriments'. They too have performed a doleful story of unfortunate and suffering love, made comic and tolerable by the presence of a 'contributory audience' in the persons, part mischievous and part benevolent, of Oberon and Puck. They have performed an unintended play, and, like the mechanicals' show, it was quite different in theatrical effect from their confused subjective experiences. They have emerged from it with more rewards than they deserve. They too have played out a literal and disturbing truth which requires the intervention of benevolent imagination to transform it into comedy and happiness.

The inadvertent actors in the wood become the conscious audience for the mechanicals once restored to Athens. If Peter Quince's company are the last diversionary interlude for a stage audience before the joy of marital completion, so the lovers themselves have played out an inadvertent interlude for the diversion of the fairies, and occupied the longer space of waiting which first gave rise to Theseus' festively impatient orders. Each group of actors has had an appropriate audience.

It needs only an easy logical extension of 'appropriate audience' to include as ideal spectators Elizabeth Carey and Thomas, son of Henry, Lord Berkeley, or whoever may have watched in their stead at the putative initial, celebratory performance. If so, they were participants with the stage audience in one of theatre's most deft and happy confidence tricks. In its own fictive content, and probably with its original audience, the play is whiling away the happiest of frustrating time-measures, those which lead from betrothal to marriage, and from marriage to consummation. From first to last it is a marriage play. Its affirmation of the joyous certainty of marriage, its preoccupation first and last with the interval when time itself is marooned between completion of courtship and marital beginning, are accompanied by two stages of dramatic interlude where things are otherwise; first in the lovers' tribulations and then in the mechanicals' play. At the moment in life when it can most afford to, the imagination glances back at the fragility of feeling, the larger, incomprehensible and potentially destructive forces, which married love must negotiate in order to achieve itself.

Athens and the wood in *A Midsummer Night's Dream* are times as well as places. The hours move at different speeds in the two places: slow-paced and leisurely in Athens, fast and anxiously in the wood. In Athens love is an accomplished fact for Theseus and Hippolyta, and time a ceremonious space before fulfilment. In the wood there is everything still to do, love's impulsive negotiations are yet to be completed, and the hours of a summer's night are urgent with compressed activity. The vantage point of the play is Athens, the place of imminent and unthreatened marriage, and hence equivalent to the situation of our first, imagined courtly audience. Athens, like the great house where the play was first acted, is a place of joyously participant spectatorship. Act V confirms the city's role and makes it more inclusive, as the contentedly paired lovers are at last drawn into the pattern; Act V also confirms the role of Athens for the real-life audience, which is drawn in to the shared experience of watching Peter Quince's play. As Harley Granville-Barker observed in his Preface to the play: 'What a wedding present! . . . there is the fitness of the fable, the play's whole tone and atmosphere, the appropriate ending.'

But the perfect wedding present has strings attached. Not even the happiest of Shakespeare's comedies, whether this play or *As You Like It*, is allowed to run its course without disconcerting reminders that the world is not always thus. The harmony of comedy is precarious. In *A Midsummer Night's Dream* Athens 'frames' the action, in the paradoxical momentary timelessness of its interlude between the end of courtship and the start of marriage. Such is the imaginative symmetry of the play, however, that the framing order of Athens is itself framed, by other orders of life, thought and being, which go beyond the conscious and chosen limits ordained by Theseus. The marriages of Act V have histories, of tempestuous courtship, antagonism, jealousy, violence and infidelity, of instability which has led with pain to this hard-won lastingness. We know of this from our own privileged witnessing of the earlier action, and we know of it from Oberon. Theseus and Hippolyta, however glancingly we are reminded of it in the fairies' accusatory quarrelling, are no exceptions in their pasts to the arbitrary changes and caprices of love, no matter how settled the mutual relationship they have finally achieved. Just as there is a past, so there is a future. These couples will be protected from its harsher possibilities by a powerful fairy blessing and the promised birth of unblemished children; we know of this from Oberon. But even Oberon cannot secure them against the presence in life of 'spirits of another sort', more malevolent and destructive than the forces which these fairies represent, and Puck's last contribution to the play is the most disturbing among a gathering of reminders that such a dimension exists. There are more things in heaven and earth than are dreamed of in Theseus' philosophy.

Shakespeare, then, makes special use of the privileged position of his first audience. It is privileged not because of its aristocratic status, and therefore its ease of complicity with Theseus' Englishness (though this undoubtedly helps), but because it shares with the newly married couples the unrepeatably secure and festive moment of marital pause. Only for a minority is that festive suspense an immediate and personal experience; although Shakespeare's Athens has three married couples and most marriage-feasts have only one, even in Shakespeare's Athens there are courtiers and masters of the revels for whom the transformative event of marriage is merely vicarious. Yet it is a rite of passage which is universally understood and endowed with magical significance. In *A Midsummer Night's Dream* it no doubt derives its special power from particular circumstances, but the play's immediate and lasting popularity is proof that everyday audiences find no difficulty in identifying with the happy vantage point of marital transition. This is just as well, because in the 'double persons' of Demetrius and Helena, Lysander and Hermia, Theseus and Hippolyta, but also in the other 'double persons' of Demetrius and Hermia, Lysander and Helena, Oberon and Hippolyta, Theseus and Titania, we see the mercurial and dangerous transitions which occur before love modulates into marriage, and in the persons of Oberon and Titania we see what can happen afterwards.

The fairy marriage

For human marriages, of course, the ceremony will lead to 'everlasting bond of fellowship'. There is no ominous suggestion that the Act V marriages will lead to quarrels and estrangements such as beset Oberon and Titania, who after all are fairies and immortals. All the same, we experience the fairies in the theatre as analogous to humanity, and it would be a strange reading or production of the play which ignored the invited parallels and contrasts between Theseus and Hippolyta on the one hand and Oberon and Titania on the other. In recent years directors have shown a growing inclination to press home the parallels (even at the price of several hairy quick-change moments) by having both roles played by the same actor and actress. Peter Brook's famous 1970 production for the RSC did this, as did Ron Daniels's production for the same company in 1981 and John Caird's in 1989. In Daniels's production, although it had several dubious gimmicks and eccentricities (the fairies, for example, were literally puppets), the doubling of roles was strikingly effective. It provided practical theatre evidence that Oberon and Titania, though more and other than normal people, are people nevertheless. Theirs is a mingled incarnation, selectively obedient to the laws and nature of humanity. Their marriage is a case in point: it is not like human marriage, but is in truth a marriage, analogous and complementary to the Athenian kind. One of the great critical questions of the play is the place we deem Titania and Oberon to have in the play's dramatic conception as a whole.

For the fairies, who are not mortal, time is consequently not finite. Their world obeys different rules of time, just as it obeys different rules of space, from those which govern humans, and the imagined nature of fairy marriage is different also. The logic of the play's imagination is very secure. Because the fairies are not mortal, and therefore not enslaved to time, for them there can be no true beginnings or endings, no fixed intervals, no calculations of hours or days. For the fairies the only time-measures which carry significance are the division between day and night, and the cycles of the moon and seasons. When more precise sectionings of time affect their world, it is because they have interfered with the affairs of mortals and been forced to borrow human time-measures. According to this selfsame logic, fairy marriage has no beginnings, either. Titania and Oberon have, so to speak, always been married. Life did not join them; death will not part them. They are the larger forces which surround and govern mortal existence. Even so, they are analogous to humanity, as all such larger forces are when the human imagination seeks to encompass and comprehend them. Marriage is one such analogue, so the play enacts a process of fairy marriage which has much in common with the human one, but free of the once-for-all intensities which characterize the human world. In the middle scenes of the play Oberon and Titania experience the same ordeal of estrangement that the lovers do, except that for Oberon and Titania even the ordeal itself is primarily borne by humans, who undergo, for example, the consequential penalty of seasonal disorder which Titania describes as ensuing from their quarrel. For the Fairy King and Queen themselves, there is a lightening element of spiteful playfulness in their alienated dealings with each other, so that even in the midst of her absurd besottedness with Bottom it is impossible to take Titania very seriously as a *victim*. She is altogether too powerful for that, despite the infatuated helplessness which Oberon has magically induced. The fairy marriage is not truly at risk, because time itself is not a threat to it. It is only a process of temporary estrangement, a reminder of the cosmic equivalences which encircle human loves and lives, and which humans can do nothing to control. And which they cannot understand, although we see Theseus attempt it.

The fairy marriage, delightful as it is as comedy, is also a very serious and important part of the play's design. Unity and disunity in marriage between Oberon and Titania are the focus for Shakespeare's presentation of ideas and themes which spread far beyond the central nucleus of love and partnership. In the complementary roles of Oberon and Theseus, and in the complementary marriages of the two 'royal' couples, we find these themes articulated.

In the two-phase structure of the play, it is important that we should see the experiences of Oberon and Titania as running parallel with the vicissitudes and triumphs of the human lovers. The casual but memorable linking of their names with Theseus and Hippolyta in jealous recollections of earlier love affairs is part of this. In the play itself we see a correspondent patterning. There are divisions, quarrels and estrangements between the lovers, and so there are between Oberon and Titania. There are transformations among the lovers, followed in due time by the restoration and enhancement of true order, and the same pattern marks the affairs of Oberon and Titania. If the lovers are suffering a trial by courtship which will lead in the fullness of time to marriage and procreation, its equivalent in the fairy marriage is the ruthless courtship of Titania by Oberon for possession, not of herself (for he possesses her already just as she possesses him), but of the Indian boy. In its own way, as a love object in the alternative sexuality of fairy marriage, this child is the equivalent of the procreative fulfilments that will come from human marriage. It is in their quarrelsome courtship for possession of a mortal child that the timeless fairies join the dance of time.

In a fashion appropriate to fairy marriage, Oberon and Titania replicate the human pattern at the end of Act IV, when the custody of the Indian child is settled (and, as I shall argue later, rightly settled – see pp. 131–3) and the fairy powers are reconciled. Because they are married already, they can only remarry, and thus reaffirm a peace from which the peace of their mortal dependents will draw its own new strength. It is appropriately expressed through dance and song, a physical rite of ordered joy.

The 'reality' or otherwise of the fairies troubles some critics, perhaps excessively. The theatre history of the fairies has in the past gone beyond the limits of defensible romantic sentimentality, and has recently produced a corresponding reaction. C. L. Barber, for instance, is inordinately anxious to wean us away from erroneous belief in fairies. 'The sceptical side of the play,' he argues, 'has been badly neglected because romantic taste, which first made it popular, wanted to believe in fairies. Romantic criticism usually praises *A Midsummer Night's Dream* on the assumption that its spell should be complete, and that the absolute persuasiveness of the poetry should be taken as the measure of its success' (*Shakespeare's Festive Comedy*, p. 140). Whilst he accepts (with some reservations as to its appropriate expression) the physical life of the fairies on the stage, Barber is intent that we should clearly perceive them as dramatized abstractions, projections into metaphoric physicality of certain superstitions or creative tendencies of the human mind. For Barber they represent 'the power of imagination', Puck 'does not really exist . . . he is a figment of naïve imagination', and we 'are not asked to think that fairies exist'. It is certainly true that no one will appear, like Peter Pan, to ask if we believe in fairies in order to save the life of Oberon, for the good reason that Oberon is fully capable of saving his own life. We do not need to believe literally in the existence of fairies in order to assent imaginatively to the reality of Oberon, Titania and their retinues, and we can do so without cautionary, Theseus-like reminders to ourselves that these delightful figures are only abstractions or personifications of qualities in a dramatized intellectual debate. If we have such problems with the fairies, we are probably experiencing larger if unnoticed problems with the other character-groups, and hence with the very nature of the play. *A Midsummer Night's Dream* makes sense only if the fairy marriage, too, is real.

Form and content in the marriage play

The rest of Barber's concluding statement is a better guide towards the view of *A Midsummer Night's Dream* which the present study will attempt to explore:

We are not asked to think that fairies exist. But imagination, by presenting these figments, has reached to something, a creative tendency and process. What is this process? Where is it? What shall we call it? It is what happens in the play. It is what happens in marriage. To name it requires many words, words in motion – the words of *A Midsummer Night's Dream*.

(*Shakespeare's Festive Comedy*, p. 162)

The statement is vague, but it takes us in the right direction. The fairies exist, in meaningful and vivid life, on the stage, but we do not expect to find them lurking in the bosky suburbs on our way home from the theatre. On the other hand, we are not going to bump into the other character-groups either, despite their more familiar kinds of naturalism. For the purposes of this drama, the courtly figures, and the lovers, and the mechanicals, are just as real and just as abstract. The idea of 'reason' represented by Theseus is just as stringently examined in the play's events as the idea of 'imagination' which may be represented by Oberon. The perils of love and surreptitious courtship are just as real when those involved meet with farcical catastrophe, as they do in 'Pyramus and Thisbe', as when they meet with comic rescue and salvation, like the lovers. Infidelity is part of the spectrum of love's pains, whether committed by Demetrius, or Theseus, or Titania. Transformative sleep, and the aberration of the wakening eye, form part of love's inexplicable vicissitudes, whether Lysander or Titania is the victim.

The play, especially as a marriage play, stands upon the separateness of its four character-groups. Each group embodies certain ideas or abstractions, but is not for that reason abstract. Their differentiated groupings allow certain ideas to meet and interact, even as the characters do, both within and between (especially between) their distinctive group identities. In recent years the knowledge that the play was almost certainly first performed at the marriage feast before an intellectual, sophisticated audience, coupled with reaction against the over-sweet romanticism of earlier readings, has caused critical emphasis to fall upon the intellectual background of the play. This is useful provided we do not forget that it is still a play, not an intellectual debate, that it is traditionally popular with audiences who do not see themselves as intellectual or sophisticated, and that its ideas are first and foremost alive *dramatically*. The collision of ideas, like the collision of character-groups, is dramatic. Even more accurately, it is dance-like. It rests on a habitual symmetry and patterning which is not primarily intellectually pleasing, like a work of philosophy, but aesthetically pleasing, like a dance. Barber is brilliantly correct to see the process of the play as 'words in motion', but we shall twist that motion out of shape if we separate the fairies from the 'human' and see their motion as distinct.

To unify the four groups – the fairies, the lovers, the court figures, the mechanicals – as partners in a composite dramatic dance is further to affirm the truth of Barber's implicit association between dramatic form and content: 'It is what happens in the play. It is what happens in marriage.' That is to say, the play exquisitely mirrors in dramatic *form*

27

as well as content the appropriate entertainment for a wedding. And its groups and figures conspire to enact a cumulative vision of marriage which is greater, more comprehensive and more challenging than is suggested by any one of its corporate members.

Song, music and dance are clearly important in the play, and do not require the formidable musical support of Mendelssohn (though one kind of valid romantic interpretation is greatly enhanced by it) or the operatic conversions of Benjamin Britten (though the play's invitation to operatic form is a good indication of its true dramatic nature). The song and dance of fairy blessing at the end of the play are a formal completion of its meaning, which is not attainable by words alone; motion itself is finally the necessary extension of 'words in motion' to enact the finale of a play where *movement* is the very essence of dramatic meaning. As the court phase of the play is closed by dance and song, as day again turns into night, so the woodland phase is closed in Act IV scene i by dance and music, as night turns into day. These are the indispensable ceremonious recognitions, at key moments in the drama, of a multiform dramatic utterance which is intrinsic to its meaning. This is considered more fully in the last section of the present chapter and in the discussion of the play's structure. Important also are the other set-piece occasions when music or dance extend the resources of language, including the comic ones: the fairies' lullaby sung to Titania will repay attention, but so does the Bergomask danced by Bottom and the mechanicals at the end of 'Pyramus and Thisbe'. The whole play will prove on examination to work in comparable musical or dancelike ways. Its art-form has the patterned reassurance of dance, the concord (and containment of discord within concord) of music, and is therefore festively appropriate for a wedding.

Opposition, transformation, reconciliation

In general we can be trusted as audiences to learn our parts at once, cues and all, and recognize the dancelike comic order within which the confusions of the play occur. If so, we shall also have no trouble in recognizing the pattern of *transformations*, of metamorphoses, which most recent criticism of the play has rightly stressed. *A Midsummer Night's Dream* is a play which is deeply concerned with opposites and polarities. Many of these are not mere accidents of plot, or formal contrasts of ideas, but opposites and contradictions which exist in human nature, and which humanity seeks to resolve most particularly through the institution of marriage. Our play's first celebratory audience, therefore, in watching *A Midsummer Night's Dream*, was watching in benign circumstances the formal enactment of conflicting forces for which marriage is a reconciliation and a resting-place (even if, as with Oberon and Titania, there may be periodic need for vows and contracts to be reaffirmed).

Broadly, these opposites are embodied in the contrasts between Athens and the wood, between the civilized and the natural world, between abstention from love and consummation of love, between day and night, between the different manifestations of desire, between Theseus and Hippolyta on the one hand, and Oberon and Titania on the other. In their movements from Athens to the wood the major characters undergo a series of significant transformations, an experience from which the inhabitants of the wood itself are not immune. Essentially, the comic-painful experience of contrariety begets transformation. In several cases these particular transformations enable fitness for marriage to be achieved, while the cumulative pattern of transformative events composes a dramatic celebration of marriage itself.

The main action of the play, therefore, in Acts I to IV, is centrifugal in nature and brings the characters involved into confrontation with a set of contrarieties. Through the comic pains and confusions of courtship these are finally resolved, and the victims of the night's confusion brought into reconciled preparedness for marriage. The action of Act V is centripetal in nature, gathering all the play's groups (and all its figures, since no one at all – except, in one text, Egeus – is omitted from the conclusive meeting at the marriage feast) in one harmonious congregation. This is not to suggest that there are no discords, or suggestions of possible discords, in Act V. There are many. At this stage of the play, however, they lack the disruptive and violent immediacy of confrontations in the wood, and are projected instead as threats to human concord which it is the work of love, expressed in marriage, to keep at bay as long as may be. Not even the walls of Athens or the hall of Theseus' court are strong enough to exclude securely or for ever some of the threats inherent in the life-risking wood of everyday existence. Some day the cloud-capped towers and solemn temples will dissolve, as Shakespeare was to acknowledge in the more embracing vision of a later play, but in the more youthful vision of *A Midsummer Night's Dream* the perils are more shadowy and subject to the powers of fairy exorcism. Protected finally by that authoritative dance of blessing which closes the play, all are safely gathered in to the security of Athens, transformed by their excursion to the wood. In Act V a harmonious simultaneity of clearly-defined groups and presences brings order and durability to the short-lived alliances, incongruous affinities and confusions of the darkness.

This is the magical symmetry of marriage which the play celebrates. Doubleness becomes singleness, as two people become one, and in becoming one, paradoxically, become freely and unpossessively two. The singleness of marriage permits harmonious doubleness as the acquisitive or dismissive dualities of love and courtship, attraction and rejection, did not. Beginning appropriately enough with the reconciliation of Oberon and Titania in Act IV, the closing phase of the play exhibits quite different ways of being two people, of enjoying the 'double blessedness' which is life's alternative to the 'single blessedness' of chastity. It is set against the singleness which earlier threatened both Hermia and Helena, and also against the antagonistic, rivalling or predatory doubleness which characterized the courtship-conflicts of the middle scenes. If Oberon and Titania are fitting inaugural presences for marital doubleness (in part because they alone are married already, in part because the latter action begins in the wood, which is their own terrain) it is taken up by Helena in what may be read as one of the pivotal lines of the play:

> I have found Demetrius, like a jewel,
> Mine own and not mine own.
> (IV.i.190–91)

In the play's symmetry (which is, essentially, not solely intellectual but emotional, physical and moral) the marital celebration of Act V can be seen as incorporating into human life the *permission of doubleness,* whereas the earlier centrifugal action of the wood can be partly characterized by *exposure of doubleness.* This distinction lies at the centre of the play's conception of marriage and extends not only to the partnerships which marriage forms but to the individual contrarieties which marriage reconciles.

Dominant amongst these contrarieties are chastity and consummation. The tension between these two, their cogent opposition of claims upon the sexual imagination, can be seen in Titania's speech at the end of Act III scene i, as she instructs her fairy retinue to conduct her adored Bottom to the woodland bedroom:

> Come, wait upon him. Lead him to my bower.
> The moon methinks looks with a watery eye;
> And when she weeps, weeps every little flower,
> Lamenting some enforcèd chastity.
> Tie up my lover's tongue; bring him silently.
>
> (III.i.192–6)

There is a certain coyness on the part of some commentators on the question whether the grotesque relationship between Titania and Bottom is ever consummated. Whatever the unknowable offstage truth, there is little doubt that when the couple next appear (in Act IV scene i) they are very well contented with the world and with each other. Whatever Titania's intentions, she is unquestionably besotted with Bottom when she gives these orders to her fairies; personal chastity (or chastity-within-marriage) is certainly not uppermost in her priorities. Therefore this little speech reads oddly. Why should Titania, at this moment when she seems rather to be bent upon committing rape than in danger of experiencing it, choose to anthropomorphize the moon and the flowers by making them shed tears for defloration? Most editors agree that 'enforcèd' means 'violated' and find no ambiguity in the expression. William C. Carroll in his observations on the passage disagrees:

The personification of the moon here seems to work in two directions. If 'enforcèd' means 'violated', then the moon mourns the loss of chastity, but I cannot see how mourning such a loss is appropriate to Titania's situation. If 'enforcèd' means chastity 'forced upon' someone, then the moon laments that sexual completion has not occurred; this reading fits the eager Titania's desires more closely. Moreover, it reminds us that marriage *does* mean sexual completion (otherwise the marriage is not legally enforced).

(*The Metamorphoses of Shakespearean Comedy*, pp. 152–3)

He goes on to draw the parallel with the chastity which was legally enforced upon Hermia at the beginning of the play as the penalty for her disobedience in refusing to marry Demetrius. In my view, the verbal ambiguity is not sustainable: 'enforcèd' means 'violated' in Titania's speech, not 'compulsory'. Yet the oddity remains. There is a peculiarly ill-timed one-sidedness in Titania's lament, given the erotic spellbound relish of her current enterprise. And we cannot be unaware that 'enforcèd chastity' in the sense excluded from the particular phrase, that of compulsory sexual abstention, has indeed entered into the play's sexual debate. It has taken the ambiguous form of an estimable penalty, a kind of virtuous defeat for the true propulsions of the flesh (and hence the very opposite of the escapade that Titania is here engaged in). That is to say, although the particular phrase gives little scope for ambiguity, the sexual vocabulary of the play quite certainly does so. The moon 'looks with a watery eye', and Luna (or Phoebe), the goddess of the moon, is also the goddess of chastity. But the moon (as we shall see in extended discussion later) is a prolific and a diverse image in the play. The moon, or Luna, is the heavenly form of the triple goddess whose earthly form is Diana the huntress, goddess also of childbirth and therefore of achieved procreation. In Ovid's *Metamorphoses*, one of Shakespeare's major sources for the play, Titania is a name for Diana (see *Metamorphoses*, III). What Paul A. Olson calls 'the paradox of a licentious goddess of chastity' may therefore be a straightforward joke about sexual incongruity and double-think, or it may be a recourse to mythological associations in order to boost Titania's status at this dubious moment. Titania's speech may not include specific ambiguity, but it does in any case voice contrary impulses of feeling which are essential to the play.

These contrary impulses are resolved and reconciled in marriage. The central point about the conception of marriage which is celebrated in *A Midsummer Night's Dream*, and endorsed by the ethical climate of the age which produced it, is that it integrates chastity and sexual fulfilment: if all the features which make for good marriage are fulfilled, then marriage embodies sexual release without the taint of spoliation, the guilt-ridden associations with the Fall, which otherwise mar the loss of innocence. The tests which such a marriage must satisfy are quite numerous; they include the felt truth of romantic love expressed through the willing consent of the partners, but they also include appropriate equivalences of age, and status, and wealth, and social position. The notion of romantic love as a private treaty between individuals, insulated from its social context, does not, in Shakespeare's mind, contain the sufficient promise of happiness that later, more ingenuous, interpretations of his work have wished to find there. Shakespeare is imaginatively sympathetic to the private intensity of condemned love; it is the central subject of *Romeo and Juliet*, a companion piece to *A Midsummer Night's Dream* in Shakespeare's development, as we have already seen. In *A Midsummer Night's Dream*, however, a necessary condition for married happiness which is finally met by the lovers is that of public fitness and approval. For this to be gained, the lovers must have parental consent to their marriage. At the beginning of the play Hermia does not have this, and its absence is a crucial element in the initial disorder of the lovers' relationships. Eventually the necessary reconciliation is achieved when ducal authority is substituted for paternal authority and Theseus overrules Egeus' opposition. These are not just arbitrary external inconveniences, which we might be wrongly tempted to see as subordinate to the priority of individual feeling. If we consider them in this way we are distorting and simplifying the complex social texture of Shakespeare's marriage play. All such matters hold equal sway, potentially ruinous or potentially benevolent, in that composite of forces which enables or forbids a marriage, and which must be negotiated before it can successfully take place. This is precisely the set of forces which is formally lamented in the love duet between Lysander and Hermia which we hear in Act I (I.i.132–49). The play engages with the many diverse threats which can overtake love on its way to becoming marriage. Once again it is appropriate to recall the situation of the two key figures at the play's first ceremonial performance – figures watching a play about the harsh negotiations of love at the very point in their lives when they were most acutely aware (we hope!) of having successfully concluded them.

If all these various conditions are indeed fulfilled – private and public, social and legal and religious – then the event of marriage does not involve the *surrender* of chastity, but the alteration of its nature and expression. Fidelity of love within a socially permitted marriage brings with it the 'permission of doubleness', and a part of this is the retention of single virtue, of single chastity, within the sexually consummated, procreative union of marriage. Marriage is pre-eminently able to harmonize the ethical polarities of human physical existence. *A Midsummer Night's Dream* is profoundly concerned with the process of winning, and losing, and holding on to, this reconciling harmony, and all the four main groups of characters contribute to its dramatic exploration.

Courtship and wedding; the two-phase structure

It is this process which accounts for the two-phase structure of the play and the separate nature of Act V. Shakespearean comedy quite regularly presents the completion of a major action some time before the end, at a point which subsequent introduction of act and scene divisions commonly places at the end of the fourth act, but this construction is particularly meaningful in this play. We have seen already how it marks the 'return to Athens', the re-emergence of the 'framing' environment of Theseus' court, rather than the active and transformative environment of the wood. We have noticed too that it is followed by ceremonial completions of the undertakings carried through with much comic trouble and difficulty in the middle scenes – the marriages that follow courtship for the lovers, and the performance that follows rehearsals for the mechanicals.

In considering the play as a dramatic presentation of marriage, we should also notice the significance of the particular time-interval which it occupies. As outlined earlier, the first phase of the play (Acts I–IV) anticipates a tedious interval of four days before a desired fulfilment, and the fifth act also begins with a gap of time to be occupied, in this case a mere three hours 'between our after-supper and bedtime'. Act V appears to take place in the last few hours of the time-interval to which we were introduced in the opening scene of the play.

The play's structure is richer and more momentous than this, and the celebratory nature of *A Midsummer Night's Dream* as a marriage play only becomes clear when the difference between these two intervals is recognized. For Theseus and Hippolyta the time between the beginning of the play and the end of Act IV marks the time between betrothal, or the completion of courtship, and the ceremony of marriage. In more disorderly and explosive forms, it marks the same interval for the lovers. The play opens with the compelled engagement of Hermia to Demetrius and with the avowal of a true if unapproved betrothal between Hermia and Lysander, which they hope to confirm by marriage when they are safely fled from Athens. After the convulsive disengagements and re-engagements of the middle scenes, the lovers have moved from a situation which we might call 'false betrothal' to one of true marriage, marked in the triple ceremony which has taken place between the end of Act IV and the beginning of Act V.

In the world of mortals, unlike that of fairies, time is finite, and the interval between the end of courtship's dispositions and the rite of marriage can be fixed and numbered in days. Even for the lovers, who jointly have so many confusions and perplexities with which to deal in this interval of time, the eventual alliances are almost settled when the play opens. There is only one exception, although its effects are far-reaching. This is the aberration of feeling in Demetrius, who has renounced his former affection for Helena and transferred his feelings to Hermia in a sudden, inexplicable infatuation. Troubling as this is, it is an instance of the instability and fickleness of love, its impulsive and irrational transfers of allegiance, as it occurs amongst *unmarried* lovers. This, as we shall see, must be set against a convention of constancy and permanence in *married* love which governs the thought-pattern of the play; we are repeatedly – even promptingly – reminded of it in the text, and of the difference that we can expect to find in the psychology of love between its manifestations in the unmarried and the married states. The inconstancy of Demetrius, which we hear of in the more or less naturalistic opening speeches of the play, anticipates and provides a precedent for the hectic sequence of equivalent changes and inconstancies which take place in the wood when the play's established comic pattern is in full control. It is important for the audience to be made aware at the outset that there is a realistic equivalent to the artificial transformations which will occur in the dream world, and it is Demetrius who supplies the link. Demetrius exemplifies the inconstancy and unreason of unmarried love within two separate conventions, and as a carefully placed figure in the comic pattern he enables audiences to enjoy the distanced artificiality of the lovers' woodland antics without the ultimate security of feeling that what happens there is mere farcical artifice, wholly unconnected with believable real-life behaviour. If once again we recall our notional 'first night' audience of newly married Elizabethan aristocrats, then it is clear that over-much convention-bound security might mitigate rather than increase the entertainment offered by the play. For such an audience the piquancy of *A Midsummer Night's Dream* might lie in watching the enactment of romantic dangers which they have escaped, and this subjective pleasure would surely be sharpened by a credible connection between the world of moonlit fantasy and the world of experience.

In the second phase of the play (Act V), the world of experience has once again come near. It begins with a brief but wonderfully effective transitional passage at the end of Act IV scene i. This passage has two crucial events. There is first of all the reconciliation and 'remarriage' of Oberon and Titania, discussed earlier, expressed in a celebratory ritual of dance and song. This dance of reunion is the only 'wedding act' which is formally represented on the stage. Oberon's reconciliation with Titania marks the symbolic restoration of cosmic benevolence which permits the ultimate achievement of human married love. This dance is a pivotal moment in the play: it completes the 'courtship' phase and inaugurates the 'wedding' phase. It is both end and beginning.

The second event of the transitional passage is the awakening from sleep of the lovers and then Bottom. All of them in turn are briefly stranded in their minds between the two worlds we have seen them occupying. For the lovers at this transcendent moment, the desperate volatilities of courtship are laid aside, and through their own corrected wills and Theseus' benevolent patronage they move instead to the settled imminence of marriage. All the waking sleepers here experience a moment of evanescent insight which is central to the play, but by its very nature it is 'momentary'.

From this point forward, as we return to Athens and the last act, the second phase of the play takes over. It occupies the second 'interval', the shorter one of three hours, which lies not between courtship or betrothal and marriage but between marriage and consummation. The events of this final act will be more fully considered in Chapter 7. In this discussion of *A Midsummer Night's Dream* as a marriage play, however, there is one consequence of the transition which it is appropriate to consider now, and this is the changed relationship between the play and the real-life audience. Like so much else in the play, the effect is 'double': it brings the audience closer in some respects to the figures on the stage, but distances them in other ways (or, perhaps more accurately, alters the basis of theatrical distancing from what we have so far been accustomed to). The second-phase position of the real-life audience is the subject of the next section.

The privileged audience

In the second phase, during which the newly married couples must somehow occupy the hours to nightfall, the play becomes consciously preoccupied with its own theatrical nature.

The audience on stage is watching a play about the tragic death of lovers, made suitable for the occasion largely because its potentially upsetting plot is performed with redeeming dreadfulness – indeed with literal dreadfulness, since the actors are so frightened of causing offence. But that is not the only reason why 'Pyramus and Thisbe' is acceptable fare for its on-stage audience. The three pairs of lovers also have the knowledge that in their own lives the perils of illicit courtship have been successfully outlived. Indeed, they can afford to be jocular in their audience response to things that threaten them no longer.

The relationship between the real audience and the on-stage audience in Act V is the core of *A Midsummer Night's Dream*'s great structural triumph as a marriage play. Although the play's structure has internal validity regardless of the setting in which it was first performed, it becomes particularly attractive if we think of it once more as a performance for a courtly wedding. The two audiences – the real and the dramatized – are brought close together and yet kept separate by a masterly display of theatrical tact and wit.

The situation in Act V, as we have seen, is that three couples are caught in the festive tension of an interlude between the ritual of weddings and the first consummation of a lifelong union. The couples on stage are watching a play and so of course are Shakespeare's own audience. Remembering the likely occasion of the play's première, therefore, we have an audience at a marriage feast watching a play about the audience at a marriage feast watching a play. Thus far there is little to choose between the two audiences.

However, the audience on stage includes those very people who have been actors in the first four acts of *A Midsummer Night's Dream*. Their presence as spectators at this festival has been gained from comic disorder. The real-life audience knows this and has witnessed the lovers' history, but Lysander and Hermia, Demetrius and Helena, remember it very imperfectly – well enough to describe some of their experiences to Theseus and Hippolyta, but only as a kind of dream. Moreover, Theseus at least is highly sceptical about it. The real spectators at *A Midsummer Night's Dream*, therefore, enjoy an advantage over the imaginary people they are watching. *We* know what *really* happened in the wood; we know what is 'true'. Therefore we know that Theseus' rational scepticism is misplaced, and we know that these happy lovers, scoffing at the tribulations acted for them by Peter Quince's company, are largely oblivious to their own very recent entanglement in situations just as fraught with possible disaster. We 'know' that what our stage audience considers untrue or absurd is really 'true'. From our privileged position, then, we authenticate imagination and dream over reason and social reality. When the play's first audience 'knew' these things, it knew within the understood conventions of dramatic fiction all about the deceptions, confusions and anguish that can waylay unmarried lovers on their way to lasting partnerships. The audience in the theatre is superior to the audience on the stage in its possession of the past. For the central figures in the courtly audience, the experience that is *shared* with the 'Athenian youth' is one of transformative novelty which is simultaneously rendering their own past dreamlike also. There is an equivalence between the past of the real-life audience and the past of the stage audience in terms of immature experience conclusively negotiated. But the real-life audience knows, far better than the stage audience does, that there are truths indeed to be found within these fictions, 'if imagination amend them'. So while the event of 'Pyramus and Thisbe' is simultaneous for its two audiences, we perceive it only in some respects as they do, because our perception of Bottom's play is filtered through our perception of his fictive audience and our prior knowledge of them.

'Pyramus and Thisbe', then, is almost a shared event, but the superior perception which distances the real-life audience will serve to separate them from their on-stage counterparts, especially in dignifying the imagination as a way of seeing. We learn to value imagination because we see the stage audience's ignorance of its power. But the *moment in time* is unambiguously shared. Our watching and their watching coincide. If we are the first audience, our wedding feast coincides with theirs; for that one hypothetical but probable audience, Act V of *A Midsummer Night's Dream* is a moment of real-life magic, when the double tracks of truth and fiction, of life and drama, momentarily coincide and intersect.

This last phase of the play can thus be seen as an extended moment, when life-time and stage-time are simultaneous. Within the ceremony of *A Midsummer Night's Dream* as a marriage play, it is the moment when marriage as *event* is transformed to marriage as *condition*. The dramatic episode draws past time into itself, holds it for the extended instant of play-within-a-play, and dispatches it again into the longer dimension of the future. Before the play itself comes to an end, the tracks have again diverged, leaving the real-life audience once more in superior possession of a fictive truth. Earlier we 'knew', as the stage audience did not, that the fairies were 'real' and had benignly contrived these couplings which leave their stage beneficiaries in such mystified happiness. (This, it must be repeated, is completely different from believing in fairies!) At the end of the play we again know them to be real, as we see them invade Theseus' palace in the night, after the lovers have unknowingly gone to bed, and dance for us a marriage blessing, one that the play has brought us close enough to share. Granville-Barker was right: 'What a wedding-present!'

Multiform comedy and wedding entertainment

It will be clear from this discussion that *A Midsummer Night's Dream* is dominated by ideas of courtship and marriage. Their presence and treatment are enriched by the hypothesis that the play was initially written for a court wedding. If this was indeed so, then many features of the plot, style and structure of the play emerge as attractively graceful forms of compliment and pleasure-giving. Above all, the form of the play isolates and intensifies our awareness of the marriage moment, the extended instant between the end of singleness and the beginning of married life, the celebratory pause which marks the wedding festival itself and which is all the more intense because its central figures wish it to be over. The *uniqueness in time* of marriage ceremony is the human experience that this play captures unforgettably, drawing it out through the resources of drama into contexts of past and future. Such interpretation of the play does not depend on the unverifiable event of such a first performance; whether or not it took place, this is still what

Shakespeare was doing, and all the support we need can be confidently inferred from the text alone. But if there *was* such an audience, the play was made for it with a special mischievous and sympathetic grace.

The nature of the play, however, invites us to consider carefully what we mean by the 'resources of drama'. In presenting this account of the marriage play, I have stressed that the comedy's festive appropriateness depends on the skilful blending of content and form. *A Midsummer Night's Dream* is a play of artifice: it is, in a wholly approving sense of the word, artificial. The play establishes its own rules for invoking our credulity, devoid of any pretence that the events are, in any realistic sense, 'credible'. The same is true of the characters. The people of the play compose an intricate and intermeshed design. We can separate the groups, and talk about them independently, more readily than we can in later Shakespeare comedies, but that is merely a feature of the play, not a weakness of it. Within the play's own artifice and convention, no one group of characters is any more or less believable than the others.

A Midsummer Night's Dream is both like and unlike Shakespearean comedy as a whole, as the discussion in Chapter 1 has shown. It differs from other plays most importantly in the question of form. Form as well as content are inseparable aspects of meaning in any play, and we separate them only for convenience. In the case of this comedy, however, what strikes us when we think of form is the play's close alliance with other forms of art. The 'resources of drama' in this instance include the resources of sound, which we especially associate with music, and of patterned movement, which we especially associate with dance.

These are conspicuous features in Shakespearean comedy generally, and particularly in the late romances which *A Midsummer Night's Dream* in various ways anticipates. Earlier I referred to this play as dancelike, and noted its aptness for transference to opera. The general resemblances of Shakespearean comedy and romance to the procedures of opera are discussed by Northrop Frye in *A Natural Perspective* (1969). He notes, for example, that in opera we are able to accommodate plots which are full of improbable and comic complications, because 'the driving force of opera is provided by the music'; there are features intrinsic to the art form which override the story. Although the medium of Shakespearean comedy is primarily language, the language works in ways which are similar to operatic music. To demonstrate this working (as I shall try to do in the following pages) frequently invites the objection that we are talking about a play, and no one would notice such details in the theatre. This is quite true if we think of isolated details, but it is also true that in the theatre we are aware of repetition, variation and structure. We do not, as a rule, consciously observe them; they happen to us. In the following chapters I shall be looking closely at many details of this kind. The spirit in which they should be approached is admirably expressed by Northrop Frye in the following passage, where he develops the comparison with opera:

> The operatic features of Shakespearean comedy are an integral part of Shakespeare's concentration on the theatrical process. Thematic images and words echo and call and respond in a way which is a constant fascination to anyone working with the text. Such repetitions seem to have something oracular about them, as though arranging them in the right way would provide a key to some occult and profound process of thought. In performance, of course, they have the same function that similar repeated patterns have in music. As with music, it would take a superhuman concentration to notice every repetition consciously ... Yet there is usually so much repetition that, again as in music, even a vague and wool–gathering listener is bound to get some sense of design.
>
> (*A Natural Perspective*, pp. 25–6)

In this study I shall argue that this is a rewarding way of thinking about *A Midsummer Night's Dream*. Already in this discussion I have agreed with the widespread view that music and dance, which are always significant features of Shakespearean comedy whenever they occur, are exceptionally important in this play. However, to take the true measure of the *Dream* it is helpful to extend both these terms beyond the literal, and not confine them to lullaby or wedding dance. On the question of dance, the cue we need was excellently given by Enid Welsford in her study of *The Court Masque* (1927):

> *A Midsummer Night's Dream* is a dance, a movement of bodies. The plot is a pattern, a figure, rather than a series of events occasioned by human character and passion, and this pattern, especially in the moonlit parts of the play, is the pattern of a dance.
>
> (*The Court Masque*, p. 331)

The essential phrase here is 'a movement of bodies'. The fairies and the mechanicals literally and deliberately dance, but all the people of the play are engaged in a patterned movement of bodies which has the effect and quality of dance. Their movements from place to place, excursion and recoil, have this effect; so do the figures formed by group movement and individual variation, separation and coming together; so do the contrasts between dignified and humiliating movement; so do differences of pace; so do changes from movement to stillness, as expressed for instance in falling asleep, and stillness to movement, as in waking; so does physical suddenness. The centrality of this dramatized balletic art form to the play is above all evident in Puck. Although the text is full of cues and clues for Puck's movement, the quality of his athleticism is entirely dependent on the director and the actor. Shakespeare did not write it, but he wrote *for* it. The text of *A Midsummer Night's Dream* is in part a brief for choreography.

In the broadest terms of all, the dancelike nature of the play can be represented by its structure, which expresses in dramatic form the process of breaking apart and coming together, of controlled and rhythmic distancing and closing, severance and contact, opening up and closing down of physical space, which is at the heart of dancing.

As I have suggested, the earlier episodes of the play can be regarded as centrifugal in nature, while the second phase is centripetal. The play begins and ends in Athens, but not even Theseus and Hippolyta remain there throughout. (The only named figure in the play who belongs wholly to Athens is Philostrate, the Master of the Revels and stage-manager of mirth.) Within the play itself, it is their celebratory excursion on a hunting party – an event which is partly a marriage revel, partly a 'rite of May' – which brings about the discovery of the lovers and the forming of the final marriage pattern. The geographical scope of their lives is widened much further by the memory of their earlier times and experiences. We hear about their premarital affairs and infidelities, and about that part of their personal histories when they were not lovers but antagonists and rivals. The play reaches out through recall of their past lives to distant times and distant places, while through direct experience it draws them together in the civilized unity of Athens. Athens is both a place and a time in this play – a place of stillness and a time of pause after lives which have been full of movement and action. Time and space are intimately linked in the pattern of their lives, as they are linked in dancing.

At the end of Act IV Oberon and Titania are reconciled, and their own renewed marriage is ritually expressed in dance and song. They too, however, in their elemental, superhuman forms, have been associated strongly with geographical distancing. In their pasts are alleged affairs in other places, but also exercises of their separate sexual roles with faithful retinues of their own (sexually homogeneous) orders, not only in a wood near Athens but in India. The globe itself has been the field of their estrangement, while the Athenian forest on a spring morning is the apt place for their reunion, confirmed in Act V by their benevolent invasion of the play's Athenian centre.

The recalled and suggested geographical ranging of the two royal couples is only the symmetrical reinforcement of the design enacted in the play by the other two groups, the lovers and the mechanicals. For Bottom and company there is a production planned and cast (with certain disagreements as to casting) in Athens, rehearsed with much confusion in the wood, and finally performed in Athens. For the lovers there are relationships and marriages arranged and cast (but again with fateful disagreements as to casting) in Athens, played out with much confusion in the wood, and finally celebrated in harmonious marital pairings in Athens. The developments of these two plot sequences will be discussed in greater detail in Chapter 3. For the moment it is necessary only to note their formal resemblances and the opportunities which this affords for one grouping to provide a comic comment on the other.

There is, then, a dancelike structure of breaking apart and coming together – represented in particular by the movement from Athens to the wood and from the wood to Athens – which includes all the four constituent groups of figures in *A Midsummer Night's Dream* in the same inclusive pattern. The form is comedic in nature and has a broad symmetry of design which is reassuringly evident to audiences. Whatever fractures or disorders may occur in the events of the play, there is never any doubt that we are party to a benevolently controlled, harmonious structure.

If the larger design of patterned movement provides a wider context for particular dances, so the play's whole repertoire of sound provides a wider context for particular music and song. Even the songs themselves exhibit the design of contrarieties; Bottom's claims to 'a reasonable good ear in music' are unlikely in most productions to be borne out by a pleasingly melodious rendering of 'The ousel cock so black of hue'. The discords of his musicianship play against the fairy harmonies to make a rich contrasting arrangement. Other opportunities for sound contribute to the play's diverse instrumentation, but the greatest variety of sound consists in speech itself. This comedy has a quite exceptional range of styles – contrasting degrees of eloquence, complexities and simplicities of language, kinds of metre and rhyme-scheme, delicacies and coarse incongruities of the spoken word, modulations and transitions of speech-tone – and they together form a composite design of verbal orchestration. Again, Puck is an interesting exemplary figure. When he puts the love juice on Lysander's eyes, to restore his former affection for Hermia, and says:

> On the ground
> Sleep sound.
> I'll apply
> To your eye,
> Gentle lover, remedy
> (III.ii.448–52)

does he indeed say it or sing it? Conventionally, he says it, but the margin of lyric definition between speech and music is at this point almost impossible to draw.

The text of *A Midsummer Night's Dream*, therefore, is appropriately treated also as a libretto for the speaking voice, a set of instructions to actors for an unusually wide range of vocal instrumentation. Its stylistic diversity is the most important single feature of the multiform artifice which establishes the play's unique convention and sets it apart – in degree if not in kind – from the other comedies. This internal variety of form, as much as anything else we have so far considered, makes it appropriate entertainment for a wedding. If Puck were not at hand to give the play a finer conclusion, the cast of the on-stage audience could appropriately have stepped forward to address the real-life audience, on that first celebratory occasion, with the closing lines of *The Two Gentlemen of Verona*:

> . . . 'tis your penance but to hear
> The story of your loves discoverèd.
> That done, our day of marriage shall be yours;
> One feast, one house, one mutual happiness.

3. The Structure of the Play

Much of a play's meaning and effect can be illuminated by looking at the way it is constructed – the internal organization of scenes, events, characters and language. In some plays the structure, or mode of composition, is very simple and straightforward, and we can talk of something as obvious as the beginning, the middle and the end; in more precise dramatic terms we can use the classical structure of exposition, complication, climax and resolution. Without a coherent dramatic structure it is unlikely that any play could work effectively on stage. Although some great plays have relatively simple patterns of composition, as a general rule we can say that great plays are structurally complex, and if we are to understand them we need to take account of many things besides the plot, or historical sequence of events. *A Midsummer Night's Dream* is structurally a very intricate play.

In this chapter I shall look at the play's structure in order to suggest some answers to two closely related questions: how is the play built up from the beginning? And how is it composed, when we stand back and look at its overall design?

The first of these questions puts us in essentially the same position as a member of the audience who has come to it completely fresh, equipped with background knowledge that anyone might be assumed to have, but no familiarity with the play itself. To see how it might work for this playgoer, I shall look very closely at the opening scene and then at the expository phase of the play, which includes the whole of the first act and the beginning of the second. Needless to say, no theatregoer could possibly be consciously aware of more than a small fraction of these first impressions, but audiences are a great deal cleverer than they know! (Shakespeare clearly had a high opinion of his audiences; otherwise he could not have written as he did. The immediate and continuing popularity of his plays confirms his judgement.)

To look at the play's overall design I shall then try to stand further back and look at features which can only become properly apparent when we know the play as a whole. Someone seeing *A Midsummer Night's Dream* for the second or third time might enjoy it more, or differently, by seeing it as a dramatic *shape* as well as a sequence of events, and this is the spectator-viewpoint I am representing in the section 'Circles and advances'. At this level, Shakespeare's dramatic ideas are an important guide for the director and the actors in deciding their interpretation of the drama and choosing an appropriate style of performance. Finally, in order to demonstrate the play's complexity of organization, I have summarized a variety of approaches to the structure. These are proposed as *co-existent*, although individual directors, actors and students will always have their own preference for the ones which seem to throw most light on the play.

The opening scene

The first scene of a Shakespeare play will almost always repay close attention, even when it is short, played by minor characters, and seemingly tangential to the action. Shakespeare requires immediate alertness from his audiences, and a good storage capacity for important clues. *A Midsummer Night's Dream* is a prominent example of significant opening statement, introducing words, images, ideas, themes and characters which will dominate the play, and unsparingly insisting from the outset on that habit of doubleness, and of truth within confusion, which are characteristic of this play's imaginative proceeding.

The scene falls into several sections, which progressively draw upon and play upon each other. First there is a private conversation between Theseus and Hippolyta; then a public and legal quarrel between three lovers and a matchmaking father; then a dialogue between two seemingly star-crossed lovers; then a threefold conversation about shifting advantages in love; and finally a soliloquy. By the end of the scene, two of the play's four social groups have been intellectually and imaginatively characterized. Meantime, the plot has been expeditiously and almost casually set in motion.

When Theseus and Hippolyta make their entrance, they begin with a duet – one of the passages of mutually supportive formal dialogue which characterize the play. This reciprocal supportiveness in the exchange of speeches is able at times to absorb estrangement and antagonism, so that sympathetic form contradicts hostile feeling. There is no hostility in this first example, but it still presents a wave-like interchange of argument as Hippolyta takes up the key terms of Theseus' complaint and returns them to him transformed to terms of consolation. The words concerned will shape the play's imaginative identity throughout: 'days' and 'nights', 'slow' and 'quickly', 'old' and 'new', and above all 'moon'. Nights, with their suggestion of unconscious time and effortless dreaming, are Hippolyta's response to Theseus' impatience with the slowly passing days before their wedding. With her understanding that time can pass at different speeds, Hippolyta introduces the temporal rhythm of pause and acceleration which marks the play's movement.

But nothing in these speeches has such implications for the play as their contrasting glimpses of the lunar cycle. The regularity of time's passage is marked by the phases of the moon, and this affects all mortals equally. Within that regularity of change from old to new to old, there is the rhythm which human beings themselves impose, the one that here divides the pair's perception of what 'four days' means. Literal astronomy, however, is only a small part of the moon's truth. One of the play's dominant images is here presented from the outset in symbolic doubleness. For Theseus the 'old moon' is a repressive human elder, parsimonious of life and wealth, and thus delaying the expenditure of love's wealth in sexual fulfilment. The moon is Luna, part of the threefold goddess: Luna (moon), Diana (earth) and Hecate (underworld). Luna, as a goddess of chastity, stands in the mind of Theseus for (at least temporary) sexual prohibition. For Hippolyta, however, the new moon of several nights hence, 'like to a silver bow/New-bent in heaven', evokes a different association with Diana the huntress, another form of the triple goddess. Diana is also the goddess of childbirth, and so the lunar image is subtly changed in Hippolyta's speech to a procreative one. (A couple with many children are traditionally described as having 'a quiverful of arrows', and the image of archery as successful fertility is not unlike that of the poet Philip Larkin, who in his poem 'The Whitsun Weddings' describes a group of newly married couples going off on honeymoon as 'an arrow-shower, somewhere becoming rain'.)

For an Elizabethan audience such associations with the moon and the moon-goddess were commonplace, available to the dramatist as a kind of imaginative shorthand. Although a modern reader may need footnotes in a text, and a modern audience will probably miss them altogether, there is still a sense of rhythmic fluctuation and renewal which we can register in the lines and intuitively attach to the impression of supportive harmony which the couple give us. The play opens with a chord, against which we hear the discords that are soon to follow.

Before they are interrupted, however, we have a brief reminder that their harmony was won from conflict. Again, this was a commonplace for Elizabethan audiences, who knew their repertoire of classical stories and would recall that Theseus gained Hippolyta by defeating the Amazons in battle:

> Hippolyta, I wooed thee with my sword,
> And won thy love doing thee injuries . . .
>
> (I.i.16–17)

This is a piece of tonal scene-setting for the coming drama, a small item in the carefully built imaginative security which will enclose the conflicts of the middle scenes. Theseus and Oberon supply differing guarantees that no harm will befall, and thus protect our assurance that it is comedy we are seeing.

In these few lines we have a formal statement like a musical phrase, and it gives us our bearings when Egeus enters and the love conflict begins. Delicately, the play adjusts to a more informal and realistic mode, and in this next stage of the scene the play is probably further from formal artifice than at any other time; dramatically, it is gradually eased into convention. The minor figure of Egeus is almost like someone borrowed from a different play. His misuse of paternal authority is the cause of all the trouble, yet this destructive exhibition of familial authority is part of that contextual social pattern which, as we noted earlier, must somehow be reconciled to any marriage if it can hope to be successful. Egeus is himself disqualified for his role by his own clear incapacity for social thought, which is why Theseus is ultimately legitimate in overriding him. The need for that eventual judgement is supplied by the characteristic vocabulary of Egeus' few speeches, which are dominated by the repetitious, egotistical vocabulary of possession: 'me', 'my' and 'mine' are the obsessive core of his utterances. They still are when we last see him (at any rate in the preferable Quarto text) in Act IV scene i, when his authority is supplanted. In the speech-habits of Egeus, legitimate parental government is translated into tyranny, and he offends the convention he appeals to. In that offence lies the spur and the final resolution of the love plot, in all those aspects which lie outside the irrationality of love itself.

Once Egeus has been placed in the containing social design, it is love's irrational proceedings which move to centre stage. Beginning at line 52, we arrive at the play's central (and, of course, finally unanswered) question: why does love choose what it chooses? In presenting the question, the play at once presents its second dominant image:

THESEUS   Demetrius is a worthy gentleman.
HERMIA   So is Lysander.
THESEUS   In himself he is;
           But in this kind, wanting your father's voice,
           The other must be held the worthier.
HERMIA   I would my father looked but with my eyes.
THESEUS   Rather your eyes must with his judgement look.
                                              (I.i.52–7)

In simplified form, the terms of the play's neat patterning are here, and are duly elaborated in subsequent speeches during this scene. There is, objectively, nothing to choose between Demetrius and Lysander. 'In himself' each is the equal of the other. Theseus' quiet language acknowledges this. It is in fact essential to the play's effect that Demetrius and Lysander should be virtually (not quite) indistinguishable from each other: their near resemblance is what enables Shakespeare to articulate his balanced argument of love. The trouble is that 'in himself' has nothing to do with the case; the social jury for love's relationships perceives a difference. Egeus, for no objective reason that he is able to give but purely it seems from arbitrary subjective preference, favours Demetrius. The provisional rationalizing term for his choice is 'judgement'. Hermia, directed solely by the deep, irrational guidance of love, prefers Lysander. Her 'eyes' determine it. 'Reason' is not a discoverable influence on either.

This reference to 'eyes' (confirmed in its suggested intricacy by further passages in this opening scene) should warn us against the simple oppositions that might prove tempting. The recurrent vocabulary of eyes and sight will be fully considered in Chapter 5, but already in this first instance we can see that there is no simple contrast of trustworthiness between external and internal data for human receptivity and choice. Apparently Hermia's 'eyes' are being identified with emotional and sensory motivations, whereas Egeus is governed by 'judgement', or maturely considered decision. Yet the self-centred emotionalism of Egeus' speech has already shown that his preference for Demetrius, though reinforced by his parental status under Athenian law, is determined merely by unrationalized caprice and owes no more to maturity, evidence or reason than does Hermia's preference for Lysander. Egeus too is directed by what he 'sees'. The line 'Rather your eyes must with his judgement look' is not therefore what it might seem, an advocacy by Theseus of rational over visual criteria for choice, but rather the imposition of one sight-mediated judgement over another. Less than a hundred lines later, in the passage of stichomythia or love duet between Hermia and Lysander, the two exchange their recognition of one of love's pitfalls in these lines:

LYSANDER Or else it stood upon the choice of friends –
HERMIA   O hell! – to choose love by another's eyes.
(I.i.139–40)

This idea is essentially identical to the first one: love's choices, whether made by lovers themselves or by authoritative figures acting on their behalf, are dependent on 'sight', but not necessarily in its literal sensory meaning.

Left alone on stage at the end of the scene, Helena, in a passage of the highest importance thematically, expresses the matter differently:

> Things base and vile, holding no quantity,
> Love can transpose to form and dignity.
> Love looks not with the eyes, but with the mind . . .
>
> (I.i.232–4)

The idea that love itself determines value, that beauty and seemliness are the product of internal organs of perception and not of the common currency of external sight, may seem to contradict these earlier passages and leave us with a simple opposition of doctrines: on the one hand, sight determines judgement, and on the other, judgement determines sight. In fact, the mystery is not amenable to such dialectical simplicity. The common term which these utterances share is 'look': both the eyes and the inner perceptions 'look'. The effect of these early passages, therefore, is to make 'sight' a complex matter and potentially confusing; we acquire a sense of 'doubleness' in questions of observation and judgement, where outer and inner perceptions transact with each other, refusing to allow us the clarity of separation. This is highly characteristic of the play's imaginative and intellectual patterning. It *seems* on many questions to be offering us alternatives and choices, and then as we draw closer it qualifies them so that they appear complementary and mutually supportive rather than good or bad, right or wrong. At best, they merge.

In this important first instance, as in so many others, *A Midsummer Night's Dream* works by *confusion*, in two senses that the word will carry: confusion as bewilderment, and confusion as a running together into single flow of separate things. This central experience of the play is already active in the opening scene, particularly in its relationship to the dominant images of 'eyes' and 'moon'.

There is another, if subordinate, line of reference to 'eyes' in this first scene, associated particularly with Helena. This involves awareness of the eyes themselves as objects of beauty. Confronting the good fortune (as it seems to her) of Hermia, who has managed to attract the adoration of both Demetrius and Lysander, Helena is anxious to explain it to herself. She finds a part of her answer in the magnetic quality of Hermia's eyes. 'Your eyes are lodestars,' she says (line 183) and in seeking to be happily infected with Hermia's beauty, and considering which of Hermia's enviable physical symptoms she would opt to catch,

she includes the eye: 'My ear should catch your voice, my eye your eye
...' Again there is something ostensibly simple which is actually double
and confusing, and the peculiarity emerges if we look at Helena's lines
more closely:

> My ear should catch your voice, my eye your eye,
> My tongue should catch your tongue's sweet melody.
>
> (I.i.188–9)

In these two lines there are three statements. The first of them expresses
approving receptivity: Helena's sense of hearing will take in the love-
charming quality of Hermia's voice. The third expresses the desire to
emulate and copy: Helena's voice will now become, in her envious
fantasy, like Hermia's voice. Between the two, pivotally balanced, is the
reference to eyes. Where does it fit into the thought-pattern? Will Helena
admire Hermia's eyes as an observer, or will her own eyes magically
replicate Hermia's? The balanced placing of the balanced phrase permits
us to read or hear it in several ways – as a choice, as a confusion, or as an
item in the cumulative dialogue between subjective and objective
experience.

   Compelled by Egeus' ultimatum but not yet placed to overrule it,
Theseus proceeds in his ducal sentence on Hermia from the polite
dispute on eyes and judgement to the fate which awaits her if she persists
in disobedience. In his first pronouncement ('Either to die the death, or
to abjure/For ever the society of men') he already commutes the absolute
severity of her father's demand by offering lifelong chastity as the
alternative penalty to death. We have looked in chapter 2 at the mergence
of chastity with faithful married love, and already in this scene we have
noticed the moon-goddess's dual role as patroness of chastity and
childbirth. Prompted here as elsewhere to be wary of alternatives in this
play, we can more readily hear the double statement of Theseus' speech
and ask if it is truly an alternative to death that he is offering.

   On one level the speech (65–78) is devoutly faithful to Diana the
goddess of chastity. The vocabulary of Christian sexual abstention
and the nun-like vocation of devotional chastity are heavily present in
the lines – 'nun', 'cloister', 'sister', 'hymns', 'blessed', 'pilgrimage',
'blessedness'. Lightly paganized for its conventional Athenian setting,
this is the Christian vocabulary of devout and virtuous self-repression.
Yet all the sanctified terms of Theseus' offering to Hermia are edged
with deterrent terms of sterility and unfulfilment: '*shady* cloister', '*barren*
sister', '*faint* hymns', '*maiden* pilgrimage' and 'virgin *thorn*', while the
lunar image is marked with the unattractive features of its chastity in

'*cold fruitless* moon'. Theseus is proffering life to Hermia if she continues to reject Demetrius, but life so presented that it mitigates but also stands in place of death. His 'merciful' alternative is a living death, and his speech invites her to perceive it as a death indeed. The whole speech is an invitation to sexual fulfilment through marriage, even if its present form has to be an emotionally unconsenting union. 'Desires', 'youth' and 'blood' are virtuous seductions to a very different religious service.

Characteristically again, the play is setting different perceptions of time alongside each other. In this sequence of speeches the play both contrasts eternity with the natural cycle of mortal life, and implicitly identifies them with each other. If Hermia opts for virginal retreat, Theseus twice tells her it will be 'For aye', contrasted with his own contented prospect, which he wants the world to share, of 'everlasting bond of fellowship' in marriage. These polar eternities are set in company with the natural cycle (implicitly abused by the stilled, non-linear condition of virginity) which is suggested by 'Grows, lives and dies' – a temporal progression which becomes eternity's equivalence. This double conception of time is fully understood by Hermia, and is echoed and accepted in her resolute answer. Mortality and eternity become almost indistinguishable human conditions, separated not by their distinctiveness as times but by the difference between linear use in marriage and virginal fixity. Yet these perspectives of enduring time (literally a 'lifetime') are linked to a specific day, the approaching wedding day of Theseus himself, when Hermia must make her choice. In miniature, in this exchange, the drama anticipates its own structure and the marriage vision it will express: marriage is 'everlasting', but it belongs ceremonially to a single day of significant choice and avowal. Before that, Theseus presides over an interval of waiting within his own accomplished courtship, during which love's negotiations must be completed by the others. The time before the 'sealing day' of Theseus' marriage is 'a time of pause', a time out of life, like no other; but it is also two separate times, for the ducal pair and the lovers, and this will be expressed imaginatively in terms of places.

This interim divergence of times is translated into the dimension of place by Lysander, when he and Hermia are left alone. With the departure of all but these two, the language changes, abandoning its introductory naturalism and moving into its many forms of artifice. The love duet between Lysander and Hermia will be considered elsewhere (see Chapter 4, 'Arias and duets') as a stylistic departure. Thematically, it strikes us powerfully as an immediate contrast with the recent emphasis on the serene lastingness of marriage, turning instead with lyric intensity to the dangerousness of love and courtship. Both natural and social dangers are lamented in Lysander's speeches and in the love duet, consisting as they do of inherent incongruities of age or status (something we are to see exemplified in comic-grotesque form later), of external impositions (something we have seen already) and of tragic natural misfortunes (something the play will finally contrive to acknowledge and neutralize through comedy). The most powerful imaginative emphasis, however, is on brevity, expressed in terms of sudden violent contrasts between darkness and light. In this passage between Lysander and Hermia, love is dimensionally separated from marriage, and some essential terms of reference are introduced for the action we are to see.

When Lysander has proposed their forest rendezvous and Hermia swears to meet him there, the language changes yet again, to rhyming couplets. For these two the rest of the scene concerns a settled purpose of romantic love, and the style accommodates itself to the emotive role-play they have chosen. The formality of this style permits the inconspicuous voicing of certain notes which might seem out of tune. The rhyming couplet may appear a rigid, formalistic device which offers little flexibility, but it can supply an unstrained partnership of the particular and the general, as it does in these surprising lines in Hermia's promise:

> ... by that fire which burned the Carthage queen
> When the false Trojan under sail was seen,
> By all the vows that ever men have broke –
> In number more than ever women spoke ...
>
> (I.i.173–6)

Dido, Queen of Carthage, incinerated herself when her lover proved unfaithful. It may seem odd for Hermia to choose this, followed by a more general scepticism about men, as part of her oath of fidelity. As a 'character' she is teasing Lysander, but with more than a trace of latent pleading underneath the joke ('You aren't going to let me down, are you?'). As the figure in an impersonal human dance, as she will shortly be, she is chorically anticipating the impetuous desertions that will test them on their way to eventual marital order.

These are perhaps the most important ways, but by no means the only ones, in which the first scene plays its decisive part in the overall dramatic structure of *A Midsummer Night's Dream*, and establishes subtle but accurate expectations in the audience.

The first three scenes: presentation of the character-groups

There are four distinct character-groups in *A Midsummer Night's Dream*, but two of them – the ducal couple in Athens and the quartet of lovers – are very closely related to each other. At the opening of the play, after the initial private interchange between Theseus and Hippolyta, and at the close of the play, before the final dance of fairy blessing, their languages are similar and concurrent, so that the two groups share their social world of Athenian court and city whilst still differing in authority and status. The first 'movement' of the play consists of three scenes in which the four groups are separately presented in their turn, and each takes possession of its corporate character and language. During this stage most of the play's important terms and ideas are introduced, with suggested variations which attach to each of the groups. The play's initial emphasis is on separateness and difference. Not until the end of Act II scene i do we see two of the distinct groups in contact with each other, and even then it is only in the insulated roles of observer and observed.

The half-exception to this separate presentation is the scene considered in the previous section, where court and lovers are brought into contact to decide Hermia's future. Although all dramatic language is governed by conventions, we are less aware of convention in this episode than at any other moment in the play. Usually when two groups meet, the language itself is the medium for a kind of music-drama in which difference of speech-modes, or hesitancy of choice between one and another, are the exact methods by which Shakespeare gives theatrical shape to his ideas. In this first encounter, however, court and lovers briefly share a common social language, one in which the artifice impinges on us less overtly than is customary in this play. The artifice is there, as we have seen for instance in the speeches of Egeus, but it does not deter us from feeling that these people can converse with each other in a mutual language, or that they naturally belong to a mutual world. As soon as Hermia and Lysander are left alone together all this changes, and the lovers adopt their own convention of language quite distinct from that of Theseus and Hippolyta, which they will all four retain throughout their transformative experiences and abandon only when they are restored to Athens in Act V. They are linguistically autonomous and united throughout the scenes of their emotional antipathies, and their community of speech corrals them within the reassuring bounds of comedy even when their emotional conflict seems most loaded with solitary pain.

The play's structure thus determines that there are four groups throughout (because the political and authoritarian status of Theseus and Hippolyta sets them apart in Athens), but Athenian differences are inconspicuous as long as propriety and order are observed in social government. The difference becomes a matter of public dissension only because of fractures between the individual lovers and between Hermia and Egeus, which bring them up against the ordering mechanism of the law. The cause of this first divisiveness then becomes a major subject of the play; perceptual fractures lie at the heart of Athenian experiences in the wood.

The second scene then introduces us to the third group, the mechanicals. While act divisions are generally unhelpful (though the Act V division is extremely convenient in this instance, accurately demarcating the second phase of the play), it is true in practice that Act I of the *Dream* contains the two 'dispatches to the wood'. A virtually identical structure marks off the first act of *As You Like It*. There, family quarrels dispatch two sets of fugitives to the transformative world of the forest of Arden, where the rules of life are sharply contrasted with the court. By the end of the second scene of *A Midsummer Night's Dream*, a promisingly ridiculous second expedition to the wood is there to lighten the seriousness of the first.

The scene is relatively uncomplicated in itself, but has its share of neatly understated connections with the opening. The last line of the first scene – Helena's promise to have the sight of Demetrius 'thither and back again' – hinted at a coming pattern of excursion and return, and this is taken up by Peter Quince's plans for sequestered rehearsal, ready for performance 'before the Duke and Duchess on his wedding day at night'. The mechanicals too will go thither and back again. Following Theseus' ultimatum to Hermia, Quince's phrase includes Athens at large, as represented by these transplanted Warwickshire artisans, in the approaching fixed occasion of the ducal wedding. The time-bounds of the play itself are again marked out by the celebrations; even the expression 'wedding day at night' interpolates another small reminder of the daily cycle that will shortly tie the play to two contrasted nocturnes. In this way the amateur producer's opening announcement links the play-within-a-play to the temporal and ceremonial structure of the comedy, as indeed does this little scene in general – not least in Quince's instructions to meet in the wood 'by moonlight'.

However, it is not mainly Quince that we hear and notice, but Bottom. Here are six people met, and the scene is a virtual dialogue. To Bottom we are chiefly indebted for such dependable briefing on the shape of things to come, though Quince takes his share of the effects. It is Quince who offers us a 'lamentable comedy', and Quince who fears distressing a sensitively credulous audience with his lion, while it is Bottom who proposes to soften the terrible effect. Between them they give promise of comic solemnity and disastrous ignorance of theatrical imagination – matters for expansive treatment later.

The mechanicals possess the play's third language to date, and the contrast with its fourth could scarcely be greater. Such is the play's linguistic richness that each of its four languages is internally subdivided into inner dialects of speech and style; this aspect of the play is considered fully in Chapter 4. Although individual voices are audible in these initial scenes, Bottom's not least among them, the primary objective at this point is to establish the collective nature of each group. Nowhere is this artistic need for 'dialect-within-unity' a more complex matter than in the first presentation of the fairies.

Audience susceptibilities must be allowed for by the playwright, and account taken of Elizabethan beliefs and attitudes towards fairies (see pp. 3–4, 102–3, 106). Official disapproval of interest in fairies (because it encouraged irreligious superstitions) and associations of fairies with witchcraft, ran alongside gossipy delight in oral and literary folklore. The blend of token disapproval and actual amusement which probably best characterizes educated attitudes is very well expressed by Thomas Nashe in a work which is almost identical in date with *A Midsummer Night's Dream*:

The Robin-good-fellowes, Elfes, Fairies, Hobgoblins of our latter age, which idolatrous former daies and the fantasticall world of Greece ycleaped *Fawnes*, *Satyres*, *Dryades*, and *Hamadryades*, did most of their merry prankes in the Night. Then ground they malt, and had hempen shirts for their labours, daunst in rounds in greene meadows, pincht maids in their sleep that swept not their house cleane, and led poor Travellers out of their way notoriously.

(Thomas Nashe, *Terrors of the Night*, 1594)

Shakespeare in fact contributed to the development of popular fairy-lore by his treatment of the fairies in *A Midsummer Night's Dream*. The miniaturization of the attendant fairies was not, as has sometimes been claimed, a Shakespearean innovation, but this play exerted a powerful influence on a generation of poets, notably Drayton and Herrick, in whose hands there grew a fashion for a fairy world of tiny inhabitants. Cobweb and Mustardseed were to shape the everyday superstitions about fairies for centuries to come, but in their own day they were one of several possibilities, some more sinister than others. The miniature is not the *rule*, even in this play. Oberon and Titania themselves are not presented as reduced in size, and Puck is perhaps an ambiguous figure, dwindling to boyish proportions from the full-scale adult size of his folklore origins. Whatever their size, there are no sinister members of this play's fairy world, but that is Shakespeare's choice.

The play's first audiences would therefore greet the fairies with uncertain expectations as to their nature. Many questions must be set in dramatic play in this scene. They need not be *answered*, because their mystique and uncertainty are legitimate parts of the play's design, but they must somehow be *acknowledged*. What is the relationship of these fairies to the human world? Are they benevolent or malicious, kindly or mischievous? How powerful are they? Will their ultimate purpose towards human beings be to damn or to bless? What kind of spirits are they? And what is their relationship to the natural world? We are seeing two groups of characters venturing from Athens to the wood. What is the wood like? And do the fairies fully represent its nature?

A close reading or a good performance of Act II scene i will show how skilfully Shakespeare gave theatrical responses to these questions, and in this the physicality and movement of his supernatural figures provide essential support for their speeches. In this way he built their composite identity (including their complex moral identity) into the structure of his play.

The initial encounter between Puck and the Fairy is very like a Shakespearean opening scene, in which essential information for the plot, and atmospheric indicators, are given by characters who may not be of first importance in the play as a whole. Act II scene i introduces a new play-world, so its function is very like that of an opening scene. Between them these two figures provide a form of 'bracketing' for the true nature of the fairy world. Puck, of course, is not a fairy, but a traditional hobgoblin whose mischievous, practical-joking nature would be familiar to most members of the audience. His presence signals a fairy world which is puzzling, humiliating, frustrating and even a little dangerous for its human victims, yet stops a long way short of evil. Certainly it is unconnected with that more alarming supernatural world which is inhabited at night by the restless spirits of the damned. For those who witness the effects of Puck's antics and are not the target of them, the results are funny. However, Puck does prefigure aspects of the fairy world which are to prove important in the play. He is a meddler, intrusive in the human world and regarding it as a proper subject for his mischievous attentions. And he makes human beings look ridiculous, or at least deprives them of their dignity:

> The wisest aunt telling the saddest tale
> Sometime for threefoot stool mistaketh me;
> Then slip I from her bum. Down topples she,
> And 'Tailor' cries, and falls into a cough . . .
>
> (II.i.51–4)

'The wisest aunt' will not be the last person we hear of in this play who comes across experiences demeaning to proud humanity and tries to explain what she cannot understand. Puck's first self-description predicts merry, but not evil, interference in the human world.

The Fairy, conversely, links the supernatural beings with the order of nature, and more especially with flowers (whose associations in the play must be distinguished from those of animals). The 'Over hill, over dale' speech predicts the appearance of fairy royalty in the person of Titania, and gives first impressions of its nature. The flowers are persons within the fairy entourage ('pensioners' or attendants, who wear sumptuous gold coats) and are garbed in the fairy counterpart of jewellery ('rubies' and 'pearls' represented by petals and dewdrops), while the fairy ring on the grass is an 'orb', associated therefore with regal sway. The immediate contribution of this speech to the play's imaginative vocabulary is a pattern of equivalences between courtly and natural value, and between human and fairy royalty: the two are different, but complementary.

Between these two 'bracketing' self-presentations, the human and natural contexts of the fairy world, comes Puck's description of the quarrel between Oberon and Titania. This is straightforward plot-setting, a preparation for the dissension we are shortly to see. At the same time, it fuses the human and the natural elements of the fairy introit; the contention is one of human counterparts, a competition between two royal personages for an attractive attendant who is appropriate to the entourage of either. Regal dignity is at stake. But the setting of this royal pleasure is natural and pastoral: with Oberon the boy would 'trace the forests wild', while Titania 'crowns him with flowers'. A further detail of fairy miniaturism, with the elves seeking refuge inside acorn cups, confirms the rapid imaginative impression of a parallel natural world.

This is the scene to which Oberon and Titania make their entry for the formal, masque-like debate and confrontation which sets and balances their opening speeches of charge and counter-charge. The rhyming speeches are immediately dropped in favour of blank verse formality, and the initial speeches are important not only for their own ceremonious interchanging masque-structure, but for the relationship they suggest between the parallel worlds. Titania accuses Oberon of a past affair with

Hippolyta, and he counters by accusing her of love for Theseus. The symmetry of charge and counter-charge, and the identity of those involved, are a transient but indispensable structural device for the play as a whole. The alternative regalities of Athens and the wood have in the past made intimate exchanges across boundaries, and established forbidden collusions of faithlessness. Yet they are now divided into appropriate unions in their own territories, even if Oberon and Titania are currently estranged (by a very different kind of jealousy). What matters is that there is no expression of malice or resentment by either of the fairies towards Theseus and Hippolyta; their antagonism is inwardly turned, and the purpose of their nearness to Athens is to bless the wedding. Titania says this at once about Oberon, while shortly afterwards we hear that Titania's fairy consort is to 'dance' in 'moonlight revels' of celebration. The fairy world is separate from but intimate with the human world, and benevolently disposed to it; this, which is crucial to our response to the lovers' trials and Oberon's meddling in them, is formally established in the ceremonious acrimony of their first appearance.

The conventions and the names of pastoral romance give an Elizabethan audience its cue, before august Athenian potentates are even mentioned. 'I know', says Titania,

> When thou hast stolen away from Fairyland
> And in the shape of Corin sat all day
> Playing on pipes of corn, and versing love
> To amorous Phillida.

> (II.i.65–8)

Pastoral romance is one of the conventions from which *A Midsummer Night's Dream* derives its form, and even in this introductory detail the association has a purpose in setting up the artifice of recreational excursion between two worlds, in temporary blendings which allow for transformative experiments in love. Oberon has deliberately and playfully engaged in transformations of the kind which we shall see him benevolently superintend when the lovers trespass into his own domain of woodland night. The Fairy King has invaded daylight. In these scenes the drama's imaginative context is being intricately woven.

These opening accusations usher in the great set-piece 'aria', Titania's speech about the seasonal disorders which their quarrelling has caused. This speech is considered in detail elsewhere (see pp. 72–5). In the structural patterning of this expository scene its place is to show the power of the fairy world to cause harm to the human world. Oberon and

Titania are revealed as the inadvertent custodians of natural forces, the source and spring of nature's realities, on which the human world depends (for much more than simply food and comfort) and which it cannot control. Dissensions equivalent to human disputes, occurring in the ungovernable places which lie outside civilized Athens, make of the fairies a centre of unsought power; order in nature depends on them, just as order in Athens depends on Theseus. Titania's speech, though it describes catastrophe, is benevolent towards humanity: she takes no pleasure in calamity.

It is characteristic of *A Midsummer Night's Dream* to set out terms for eventual harmony and union, even in the midst of dissension and anger. Since Oberon and Titania are presented as figures of potency for human life, it is important that they too should reveal this pattern. Their inauspicious meeting in the wood follows travels which have brought them both from India, where Titania has gossiped 'in the spicèd Indian air by night' with the mother of her changeling boy. This mother, though human and mortal, was a 'votaress' of Titania's order, which seems to have been dedicated to chastity and abstention from the company of men (including Oberon), but also procreative, with the pregnant votaress delighting in her fecund, swollen belly. Since Titania is a name for Diana, goddess of chastity and of childbirth, this double association would be fitting and the changeling child's dead mother an appropriate votaress. (In this way the speech represents in vivid miniature the double preoccupation with chastity and fertility throughout the play.) The word 'votaress' recurs, though, in Oberon's speech describing his discovery of the magic flower called 'love in idleness', and the 'votaress' in this case is an ideal of abstentive chastity, representing as she does a complimentary depiction of the Virgin Queen. Even as he recalls the idealized maiden votaress, however, Oberon is plotting to use the flower in order to stir up sexual love. The two speeches, seemingly so divergent in mood and intention, have fundamental ideas in common, and the effect is to unify Oberon and Titania even in their seeming antipathy. The correspondence extends even to the setting of each idealized memory at night-time by the sea. The terms of their division predict their eventual unity.

The formal exposition of the play's four character groups is completed when Demetrius and Helena make their entry. By this stage, as we have seen, a set of parallels, equivalences, connections and interactions has been established, and the audience has been alerted to certain expectations which exclude some possibilities (such as fairy malevolence) while awakening others. Although the last part of the scene is chiefly a pulse of the main plot-development, it interacts dramatically with the fairy quarrel by its emphasis on very different forms of movement.

In the fairy exchanges, confirmed especially by the orders that Oberon gives to Puck, the stress has lain on wandering, on meeting and on speed. Puck's first question to the Fairy was 'How now, spirit; whither *wander* you?' and the reply

> I do *wander* everywhere
> Swifter than the moon's sphere . . .
>
> (II.i.6–7)

Puck himself acknowledges the Fairy's recognition with 'I am that merry wanderer of the night', and when he has successfully completed his errand for Oberon he is greeted with 'Welcome, wanderer'. The errand itself has been accomplished with a speed to match the Fairy's:

> I'll put a girdle round about the earth
> In forty minutes!
>
> (II.i.175–6)

The effect is of rapid, free and globally-enfranchised movement, sustained by the exotic reference to distant India. There are, so to speak, two dimensions of excursion in the play: that from Athens to the wood, which is the discursive reach of mortals (though, as befits those alleged to have had love affairs with fairies, Theseus and Hippolyta have more far-flung histories), and that from the wood to the world, which is the fairies' privilege. This zestful liberty of movement is present in the fairies' speeches, and its counterpart is emphasis on meeting. Because of the nearby royal wedding, the wood near Athens has become an inadvertent rendezvous for the fairy world. The Fairy, who is Titania's servant, meets Puck, who is Oberon's. Puck warns the Fairy against a royal meeting, recalling that nowadays 'they never meet' without quarrelling. Titania's 'seasonal disorder' speech confirms the truth of this. Her 'order' has gathered in many kinds of place in recent times, but always to meet with and be unwelcomely disturbed by Oberon. The effect, then, is of swift and globally wide-ranging movement, broken by encounters and collisions when they are 'Ill met by moonlight'. The fairies' movement is both vast and localized, both free and confrontational.

Demetrius and Helena, too, have a specific movement pattern. Its characteristic words are 'follow' and 'pursue'. Their movement is also fast, but different in quality. Role reversal at this point humiliates both the lovers: the female is the pursuer, the male is the hunted, and the situation is demeaning for them both. The physicality of fast, unseemly movement is to a large extent responsible for its being *comically* demeaning. Running, pursuing, hiding, fleeing, drawing and spurning – all of which are physically enacted in this scene – will be evident in the bewildered antics of the lovers throughout the woodland scenes, even when they are still, even when they are face to face, arguably even when they are sleeping. What is established in this first woodland encounter is predictive in its physical quality. In Act II scene i, therefore, there are two contrasting episodes of movement: the first completes the exposition of the play and the second begins its central action.

Circles and advances

The movement of the lovers in the central scenes provides a kind of pattern for the overall structure of the play. In this section I shall consider first of all the shape of the lovers' woodland action, and then of the play as a whole, as dramatic approximations to dance.

Aside from literal dances, nothing in the play is so evidently dancelike as the woodland trials of the lovers. To see the structural importance of these episodes, it is essential to accept that the shaping of events is not simply a way of conveying meaning; rather the shape itself *is* meaning. Also, the shape is indivisible from movement and invites Yeats's question, 'How can we tell the dancer from the dance?' In the four lovers we see a sequence of figures in action, but the total sequential action of their changing experiences in the wood constitutes a single occurrence. We experience it as a succession of events in time, but also as a single event in space. Abnormal rules of time and space apply to events in the wood, and the lovers are bound by them.

In order to appreciate the shape of action, three things are crucial: the situation before the play begins, Oberon's intervention, and Puck's error. The first provides the precondition for the dance to end where it began; the second is benevolently directed to that end; the third delays and complicates it, creating farcical mistakings and allowing duplication of experience.

Before the play begins, Demetrius has been in love with Helena. There has thus been a predramatic stage when, Egeus or no Egeus, the lovers were correctly paired. In the semi-realistic world of Athens, this symmetrical pattern has been broken by erratic and irrational transference of love. The play's convention of sudden and magically-induced transfers of allegiance is not an aberration confined to the wood. It has its prototype in the 'real' world.

When the play begins, therefore, we have a group of three and a solitary. Lysander and Demetrius both love Hermia, and compete (even while still in Athens) in equivalent and patterned speeches of rival claim. Speeches, and relative positions in the group of four, are equivalent to movements and positions in the dance, and at this stage Helena is treading a figure of her own.

The stasis of this unsatisfactory position is changed to movement with the flight to the wood, taking on the characteristic 'run-and-follow' movement that we considered in the previous section. The dance now has fixed positions of allegiance, and rules of movement.

The first change is caused by Oberon's intrusion and Puck's mistake. The men are now pursuing the wrong partner. The women's positions of allegiance remain unchanged throughout; only their compelled adherence to the rules of movement changes. The men, however, change both. The wrong allegiance of Demetrius to Hermia is now matched by Lysander's wrong allegiance to Helena. In consequence, the rules of movement now include all four. Previously, Helena was pursuing Demetrius, who was fleeing from her but pursuing Hermia (and Lysander), who were fleeing. After Puck's error, Helena is still pursuing Demetrius, Demetrius is still fleeing from her and pursuing Hermia, Hermia is still fleeing from Demetrius but is now also pursuing Lysander, and Lysander is now fleeing Hermia and pursuing Helena. The change of fixed positions calls the rules of movement fully into play.

The second change is caused by Puck's first correction, the restoration of Demetrius' love for Helena. Again, as in Act I, we have a group of three and a solitary, but Hermia is now the solitary instead of Helena. At this stage both the women have undergone the experiences of double love and double rejection. Both men have now been in love with both women. At the height of the quarrelling a further complication of reversal takes place, with former friendship turned to antagonism between Lysander and Demetrius, but also between Helena and Hermia. The new allegiances, together with the disrepair of old ones, cause further movement patterns of advance and retreat, flight and pursuit, and mutual seeking.

The third change is caused by Puck's second correction, the restoration of Lysander's love for Hermia. At this point the dance is complete. The positions of allegiance are restored to what they were before the play began. Consequently the rules of movement lapse, and the speed of physical cross-positioning is replaced by undisturbed sleeping. The sequential pattern has described a circle.

The action of the woodland lovers is a patterned dance, then, and it is also a play-within-a-play. Arguably there are not one but two plays-within-plays in *A Midsummer Night's Dream*, and the fact that one is explicit and conspicuous should not debar us from noticing the other. In Act V, when Theseus is wondering how to while away the hours to bedtime, he calls for Philostrate, his usual 'manager of mirth' to provide 'masques', 'dances' and 'music' – or a play – to entertain the court; and what he gets is a play about the anguish of divided and unfortunate lovers, but so performed that it is indeed more fitting for a wedding than a funeral. Philostrate is present at the beginning of the play also, and under similar instructions:

> Stir up the Athenian youth to merriments
> Awake the pert and nimble spirit of mirth.
>
> (I.i.12–13)

Almost as if on cue, a few moments later 'the Athenian youth' makes its appearance in the persons of the quarrelling lovers, who will proceed, in the middle scenes, to act out a comedy for the real-life audience (and for Oberon and Puck). Attention has been drawn by many critics to the parallels between the 'tragical mirth' of 'Pyramus and Thisbe' and the trials that the lovers undergo (and so imperfectly remember). It is quite in keeping with the compositional technique of *A Midsummer Night's Dream* that the play-like nature of the lovers' own performance should be a part of its design.

There is a self-contained quality about the lovers' action in the central scenes. Indeed the lovers themselves are a detachable component of the play. The performance history of *A Midsummer Night's Dream* is scattered with records of productions where the lovers have been removed altogether, not least because many people have found them infuriating. Condemned for silliness, or lack of character, or romantic excess, they have been ruthlessly excised, leaving the other three groups in sole possession of the play. Whether this is an act of critical discernment or of vandalism need not concern us here, but what is significant is the ease with which the excision can be made. It requires only a simple series of cuts and a little rearrangement to remove the lovers altogether, leaving behind a very different but perfectly coherent play. We could infer from this something of Shakespeare's technique in writing the play, and make unprovable guesses that the lovers, though no doubt designed from the beginning to have their place, were grafted on to the rest at a late stage. This would not be altogether unlikely in the case of a play which specifically consists of discrete character-groups, and concurrent plot-developments which do not formally touch each other. All these possibilities, however, are more plausible if we treat the lovers as performers in an inadvertent play. Their separateness, and the clear demarcations of their language as well as their dance-action in the middle scenes, seem designed to make it easy for an audience to offer them a unitary response. Moreover, the separate doings of the four character-groups would be even more pronounced if we took no account of their role as audiences. It is obvious that the only contact between the three wedding couples and the mechanicals is as audience and players; obvious, too, that they are a very interventionist audience, well-behaved perhaps by Elizabethan standards but extremely rude and unruly by ours. The lovers' contributions to their role as audience gain added piquancy, however, from their own recent performance as unknowing actors for the audience of Oberon and Puck, a more effectively interventionist audience than they themselves contrive to be.

There is a fine shade of critical definition to be noticed here, which implicitly says much about the dramatic method of *A Midsummer Night's Dream.* In Chapter 2 (see p. 20–22) I related the lovers' performance of an unintended play to Shakespeare's imaginative location of marriage in a context of theatrical place and time; on that level it is an event in the plot, generating irony and comedy from the lovers' subsequent obliviousness to their own absurdities. However, it is also a more formal contrivance of dramatic structure. The sequence in the wood does not merely *resemble* a play (and thus provide amusing behavioural contrast with 'Pyramus and Thisbe') or become *treated* as a play (by the clandestine audience of Oberon and Puck). It *is* a play, detachable in audience response from other, contemporaneous events, and interchanging meanings by the device of dramatic coexistence. The lovers' play-within-a-play thus interacts with Bottom's activities in two separate places and times – not only with 'Pyramus and Thisbe', but with Bottom's own nocturnal interlude with Titania.

In the celebrated example of *Hamlet,* Shakespeare used the play-within-a-play as a device for placing the audience-on-stage under trial by ordeal, giving Claudius a traumatic vision of his own crime and sin, and causing him by his reactions to reveal his guilt. In the plays of Shakespeare's contemporaries the device is used for similar purposes, and is especially employed – in the form of masque and amateur performance by courtiers – as a means of punishing wickedness and exacting revenge, not merely of demonstrating wrongdoing. The finest examples occur at the end of Kyd's *The Spanish Tragedy,* Tourneur's (or Middleton's) *The Revenger's Tragedy* and Middleton's *Women Beware Women.* For Shakespeare, however, its main interest clearly lay in casting light on the play's main action and main characters by presenting disconcerting theatrical parallels, eroding dignity as well as eliciting truth. To achieve this end he usually preferred the 'mirroring' sub-plot rather than the play-within-a-play. The Falstaff scenes in *Henry IV* Parts 1 and 2 serve this purpose, and Shakespeare's supreme achievement in this regard is the Gloucester sub-plot in *King Lear*. The mirroring sub-plot has advantages over the play-within-a-play in allowing a more extensive and sustained parallelism, and in universalizing the action as a whole, making it not so much an individual history as an aspect of the human condition.

In the lovers' ordeal in *A Midsummer Night's Dream* we seem to have an early version of the sub-plot. The term is not available for use in quite the customary way, because this play is such a careful arrangement of separate character-groups and parallel histories that it is not possible to say what the *main* plot is. Nevertheless we can see that the interlocking dramatic technique provides us with equivalents of both the play-within-a-play and the reflective sub-plot as Shakespeare used them in other plays. The conventional play-within-a-play, 'Pyramus and Thisbe', presents a disconcerting theatrical parallel with the woodland activities of the lovers, providing an extreme example of the accidental comedy latent in romantic sententiousness. The 'sub-plot' of the lovers in turn provides a more extensive theatrical gloss on the antagonistic and irrational features of human, and indeed fairy, love, and the unconvincing efforts made to rationalize and order it, which characterize the play as a whole. In this general unstable situation of conflict and attraction, marriage is shown as the one successful kind of ordering, and its ceremonial fulfilment in Act V is prefigured by the harmonious completion of the lovers' dance.

The 'universalizing' quality of inset drama, in the two forms of play-within-a-play and 'sub-plot', works in *A Midsummer Night's Dream* to support the play's inclusive statement about irrationality and reason, illusion and truth, love and marriage. The lovers' action in the wood is able to take this key place in the overall design largely because of its relative insularity within the structure, and its dancelike pattern.

The lovers' play not only supports the *Dream* thematically, but replicates its overall dramatic method. Like the love dance, the whole play can be understood as an interaction of aesthetic shape and sequential movement. The extreme physicality of the play, its constant dependence for effects on contrasting kinds of movement from the actors, is closely aligned with the abstract shape of the dramatic experience as we see it in retrospect when we leave the theatre. Again parallel is with dancing, and with the dance as an entity composed of movements existing both within and outside time.

As with the lovers' plot, the play as a whole provides the preconditions for its eventual outcome in the circumstances we meet at the beginning. The whole play anticipates from the first speeches the marriage ceremony which concludes it. Although there is potential for immediate disorder (for example in Theseus' initial inadequate response to Hermia's dilemma and in the scope for error contained in Oberon's commands to Puck), there is also unquestionable benevolence of intention on the part of both Theseus and Oberon; in their separate dimensions of existence, each looks through conflict to harmony. Before this can be achieved, however, there are mistakes, delays and complications affecting the lovers, the mechanicals and Titania, and there are duplications or parallels of experience between these various groups. That is to say, the inner pattern for the 'love dance', as formulated at the beginning of this section, largely coincides with the outer pattern of the play.

The sequential movements in time of the lovers are of three kinds. The first is the circle, represented both by the recovery of symmetrical allegiances and by the physical movement from Athens to the wood and back again. The second is the direct line of flight and pursuit. The third, and arguably the most important, is the pulse-like movement of approach and recoil, meeting and parting, separation and collision, which is duplicated with a kind of spatial grandeur by the fairies. As this last example illustrates, these forms of sequential movement are visible in other groups. The circular movement, from Athens to the wood and back, is enacted by Theseus and Hippolyta on their May Day hunting party and by the mechanicals for their ill-fated rehearsal, as well as by the lovers, and both these groups exhibit the direct line of movement in their purposeful excursions from Athens.

This set of 'movement shapes' is equivalent to the patterning noted above. In finally satisfying the immediate expectations of harmonious marriage, and in ending as it begins (in Athens), the play is circular. In sustaining the promise of eventual benevolent guardianship set up by Theseus and by Oberon, the plot moves with assurance under the protective conventions of comedy to its final happiness. In presenting intermediate complications, most vividly when the crossing of group boundaries brings Bottom and Titania together, the plot displays the pulsating collisions and separations which are physically evident in movement. *A Midsummer Night's Dream* is both plot and design, an event both in and outside time. The effect is of chaos encompassed by order. But the circle of order still has danger present on its outer rim, as I shall discuss in Chapter 7.

The structural image of the circle can be extended still further. An attractive and convincing way of approaching the play's circularities has been admirably expressed by David P. Young:

In *A Midsummer Night's Dream* . . . the opposing worlds seem to form concentric circles. At first, following the characters from Athens to the woods, we may feel that the two areas are simply adjacent, but as Theseus and daylight re-enter the play, we realize that it is possible to enter the woods and re-emerge on the other side into human society. Thus, Theseus and his world seem to envelop the world of the woods. But Oberon and Titania, as we learn early in the play and are reminded directly at the end, are not the subjects of Theseus. Their awareness exceeds his, and their world is larger, enveloping his; he is their unconscious subject. Thus we discover another and larger circle, enclosing the first two. Then comes Puck's epilogue, which reminds us that everything we have been watching is a play, an event in the theatre with ourselves as audience. Here is a still larger circle, enveloping all the others.

(*Something of Great Constancy*, p. 91)

The representation of the play's action as a centrifugal and centripetal one provides us with an effective means of synthesizing its characteristic component movements into a single dramatic conception which is unique to this play, as it gathers together all the more localized analyses set out above. The play is composed of dynamic excursions from a magnetic centre followed by a counter-action of return, recovery and reunion. Conceived in this way, however, the play is finally incomplete. Puck's final words leave us with a moment in time of magical equilibrium, which is the point of balance where single life ends and married life begins. The house is hushed and still, the humans and the fairies are under one roof, day and night are harmonized. This concluding moment of festive completion only suspends, however, and does not resolve the play's innermost vision, namely that there is not one centre but two. There are two powers in the play, Theseus and Oberon, and two worlds that they represent – the city and the wood, the day and the night, the reason and the imagination. The centrifugal and centripetal forces of the play are not of one kind but two. Is Athens indeed a refuge from the wood or is the wood a refuge from Athens? Is Athens the centre, and the wood its wild and dangerous surroundings, or is the wood the centre, somehow containing Athens within itself, and the world at large its wild and dangerous surroundings? Is reason or imagination the final court of appeal for human sanity and safety? At the end of the play, *A Midsummer Night's Dream* has brought its double centres into momentary balance with each other, but only for one night, only for one theatrical moment. Oberon's presence, and that of the fairies, is temporary. The fairies, unlike the other three groups, have not completed a circular pattern of excursion and return within the time-bounds of the play. The audience is left with a moment's resolution, but a context of time where things are magically unresolved. This brings us to the play's intellectual method and its set of oppositional ideas (see Chapter 6). What this section has attempted to do is to show the theatrical structure which Shakespeare contrived with such skill and subtlety for their expression.

Summary of structural patterns

To conclude this chapter it may be helpful to summarize the play's main structural patterns. *A Midsummer Night's Dream* is structurally complex, particularly in making concurrent use of many patterns. Individually these are often clear and apparently single, but they play against each other to produce intricate effects. No one pattern, therefore, can purport to 'explain' the play, but all of them can help us to understand it and to move closer to its composite design. In particular, they are immensely helpful to the director because they help to determine appropriate acting styles, to highlight moments of significant development, to distinguish separate kinds of artifice, and to define a context for individual speeches and passages of dialogue. What follows is only one possible outline, and it does not claim to be exhaustive.

— The play has four, clearly defined character-groups. The groups appear in three different ways: (1) as homogeneous groups when no others are present; (2) in overlapping contact and direct exchange with another group; (3) as actors or audiences for another group, the audience being either public or hidden.

— The play is set in two locations, each with its own potentate. It is 'framed' by scenes set in Athens, where figures are largely in a condition of stasis, and within the 'frame' is the wood, where figures are largely in a condition of dynamic alteration.

— The play consists of two phases. The first (Acts I–IV) is the 'courtship' phase, which for Theseus and Hippolyta is the interval between betrothal and marriage. The second (Act V) is the 'wedding' phase, which for Theseus and Hippolyta (and the lovers) is the interval between marriage and consummation.

— Each phase of the play contains a play-within-a-play, or its equivalent.

— The play consists of an expositional phase (from the beginning to II.i.187) during which the four groups are separately presented and each linked to its own central preoccupation, followed by a phase of complication and confusion (from II.i.188 to the end of Act IV), followed by a phase of clarification (Act V) during which the groups are disengaged and resume the degree of closeness to or distance from each other that they had at the beginning. (In this as in other respects, it is helpful here to compare the dramatic practice of *A Midsummer Night's Dream* with *As You Like It*.)

— The play has interlocking practices of spatial placing and of movement. The movement is alternately centrifugal and centripetal in nature. The movement is complicated by the existence of two centres, Athens and the wood, and two zones of wandering, the wood and the world. Athens *appears* to be the primary centre in terms of plot, but not in terms of the play's dialectic.

— The worlds of the play may be convincingly pictured as alternative centres, as complementary centres, and as concentric circles (with an outer circle, or further world, formed by the audience).

— The character-groups are presented in a hierarchy of status, which is identified with their relationship to audiences. The lowest status belongs to Bottom and the mechanicals; they are observed by all the other character-groups, either in rehearsal or performance, and also by ourselves, the theatre audience. The lovers have higher status and are observed by Oberon and Puck, and by the theatre audience. Theseus and Hippolyta are 'watched', and watched over, by Oberon and the fairies, though not cast as theatrical performers by them, and they are observed also by the theatre audience. Titania is observed by Oberon and Puck, and by us. Only Oberon and Puck are audiences who themselves at no time have an audience, except in the theatre itself. In its self-reflexive mode, measuring status by theatrical gradations, the play grants highest rank to the Fairy King and to Puck. In short, there are several structural criteria which deter us from accepting Athens and the court of Theseus as the measure of all else.

4. Character and Language

A Midsummer Night's Dream is a play of many languages. Not all commentators have seen this as a virtue. The play's stylistic multiplicity has been condemned at times as a sign of immaturity, of inadequate or unequal revision, of artistic indecisiveness. Since this is an early play, there is no reason for instantly ruling these objections out of court. The languages of the play need to be considered on their merits and defended, if indeed they are defended, on the grounds that they serve an artistic and dramatic purpose – that the play is better off with them than without them. This section will consider the languages of the *Dream* therefore, as parts of a dramatic statement, and especially as the dramatic equivalent of a libretto in a play which touches hands with other forms of art. The bulk of critical objection has been directed at the language Shakespeare gives to the lovers, and this will be given particular attention in the following pages.

The technical variety may be briefly noted. There are the blank verse iambic pentameters which represent the characteristic formal verse of Shakespeare's maturity. Such passages of blank verse sometimes end with a rhyming couplet. The iambic pentameter also occurs in speeches made up wholly of rhyming couplets, and occasionally in quatrains (for example, Lysander's first speech when he arrives in the wood with Hermia, at II.ii.41). The other main form is the trochaic tetrameter ('Now the hungry lion roars'). Like the rhyming pentameters, this form is normally set in rhyming couplets, but occasionally in quatrains. Very occasionally there is also a two-stress line ('On the ground/Sleep sound'). It is not commonly noticed that the character who ranges most freely across these heterogeneous verse forms is Puck. The significance of this, and of Puck as an individual, will be considered in a separate section. Additionally, there is the prose of the mechanicals and the various forms of rhymed verse used in their play. Finally, there are the songs.

Within the verse forms, the nature and quality of language itself varies. The same verse form is capable of accommodating extreme artificiality and extreme naturalness, comedy and seriousness, economy and prolixity, impetus and slowness, abstraction and concreteness, closeness to and distance from a sound of individual voice and character. Shakespeare's repertoire of languages is matched by the range of demands he makes on the individual items in his stock.

This could produce a deterrent effect of sheer linguistic disorder. Perhaps it suggests irresponsible experimentation and linguistic showmanship on the part of a young dramatist more intent on advertising his diverse skills than on blending them all into a unified dramatic whole. The argument of this study is that *A Midsummer Night's Dream* is a highly unified and very subtle play, which does more than just make divergent effects compatible with each other. However, it must be stressed that the question of the play's linguistic diversity, and the extent of its success or failure in making a whole out of its very assorted parts, is the most long-standing and recurrent area of critical debate about the play.

The languages of the play have to serve a number of purposes. They separate the four character-groups, giving each its characteristic forms of statement, enabling us as audience to make clear and fluent transitions, aural as well as visual, from one set to another. They separate figures within the groups, allowing Shakespeare scope for individual characterization when he wants it and overriding it when he doesn't. They allow for kinds of utterance which (whilst not necessarily disconnected from our sense of individual characters or groups) make larger thematic statements which deeply affect our sense of the play as a whole and of its cumulative meanings. Finally, they form a composite music and a directive for the language of physical movement. In this section I shall consider the language of each group in turn (taking Puck as a special case) in relation to these needs and purposes, beginning with those speeches where meaning and form go beyond the character-group and serve to generalize our experience of the play.

Arias and duets

In his introduction to the New Penguin Shakespeare edition of the play, Stanley Wells comments: 'Several major speeches in this play are important not because they further the action or elaborate a character, but because they represent an explicit verbal development of ideas hinted at in other parts of the play. They are as it were arias in which snatches of melody heard elsewhere are fully developed.' C. L. Barber describes them as 'autonomous bravura passages' (*Shakespeare's Festive Comedy*, p. 148) and 'beautiful bravura speeches', which 'can serve as an epitome of the metamorphic action in the play': they celebrate the reach of imagination into the cosmic surroundings of the action, and its power to transform. David P. Young describes them as 'panoramas', drawing attention to their custom, and the play's, of elaborately picturing scenes which take us outside the confines of Athens and the wood and 'create perspective and distance, both in the geographic and aesthetic senses of those words' (*Something of Great Constancy*, p. 80).

Not only the expansive, lyrical and partly decontextualized speeches of individual characters serve this function in the play; so, characteristically, do 'duets', the passages of private, balanced and reciprocal exchange between two speakers. They may be composed of formal antithesis and contradiction, in which the aesthetic effect is a total one of double truth and equipoise of vision rather than of disagreement; the first two speeches in the play, by Theseus and Hippolyta, are an example of this. Or they may be structured on a pattern of reiteration and intensification, in which the reply accepts and emotionally deepens a formal proposition contained in the first speaker's utterance; Hermia's replies to Lysander in their early generalized lament for doomed love follow this pattern. In another variety, the second statement of the duet may pick up and extend the imaginative, and perhaps the geographic and spatial, reach of the first. Whatever their adopted form, the careful artifice of double statement takes them into regions of thematic generality which overlie their local circumstantial meanings.

One of the most important 'arias' of the play is Titania's speech about the blighted seasons (II.i.81–117). Titania and Oberon have only just met in the play, and after their balanced duet of jealous mutual recrimination Titania describes the consequences of their quarrel for the human world (see pp. 58–9 for discussion of the context of this speech). It stands alone as an evocation of disorder in which the natural and the supernatural, the human and the extra-human, merge and become inextricable. Alexander Leggatt notes about the speech: 'As in the final song of *Love's Labour's Lost*, the workings of nature provide a common ground of experience: the fairies discuss a world familiar to the audience, and for a moment they seem closer to us than any of the mortals have been' (*Shakespeare's Comedy of Love*, p. 107). It is true that suddenly we are in the real world, so real that the speech has been seen (and used as evidence for dating the play) as a topical reference to the cold, wet, miserable summers of 1594, 1595 and 1596. The topical reference is virtually certain, but the effect is twofold. One, as Leggatt suggests, is to bring the fairy world very close to the audience's everyday experience; the other is to place that experience in a frame of adventitious and inscrutable disorder, the arbitrary world of 'acts of God' in which humans have no option but to live.

In Titania's vision the fairies and their quarrel become a metaphor for human comprehension of the world. They are humanized, provided with equivalents of human dissension in the form of estrangement, jealousy and rivalry, together with that magnetism of natural and necessary partners which makes the estrangement unendurable without the indirect relief of physical quarrelling. Here as elsewhere are suggestions that it is literally unnatural – a breach of nature – for Oberon and Titania to be parted. The disorder caused in the cosmos, represented especially by the moon's anger, is a magnified equivalence of disruptions caused by human upheavals in marriage. The misery of the weather is likewise unnatural, a breach of the norm. It is only by such humanized metaphors that human beings can personify and explain to themselves the eruptions of chaos in a cyclical order of seasons and weathers which, when it obeys the customary cycle, they perceive to be benevolent.

Titania affirms the rightness of the underlying human vision, because she is indeed benevolent. The speech is rich in its articulation of values; it humanizes and moralizes the working of the natural surroundings which the fairies govern. Rhythmic succession and the natural bounds of place are central positives in the speech: the seasons should respect their given character, and when they do so there are rituals to sustain them. It is not winter hardship, but winter-in-summer, which is wrong; winter itself, in this pagan dramatic fable has its religious consolation:

> The human mortals want their winter cheer.
> No night is now with hymn or carol blessed.
> (II.i.101–2)

It is not the tides or the rain, but the unseasonal excess deriving from lunar fury, which causes 'rheumatic diseases'. The seasons, servants of these royal nature-spirits, are here as elsewhere royalized in natural costumes and change their 'wonted liveries' of service. Procreation, childbirth and fruitfulness are images of benign order, beautifully expressed in 'childing autumn', but the pivotal word 'increase' transfers the comeliness of timed fruition to the chaos of unpredictable, disordered generation, and hence a 'progeny' of evils. Titania evokes in revulsion a world of what we now call mutants, and finally unites herself and Oberon in the guilt of parentage. A little-noticed detail of the speech, yet one which no critical discussion of Shakespeare's image patterns should neglect, is the Queen's reference to the anger of the winds that blow to please and serve them:

> Therefore the winds, piping to us in vain,
> As in revenge have sucked up from the sea
> Contagious fogs . . .

> (II.i.88–90)

This is a powerful image of disregarded music. The piping winds are a harmonious equivalent in the world of nature to the human arts of ordered, pleasing sound, turned to disorder by dismissal and neglect. The ceremonies of courteous acceptance have their counterparts in nature; there are interchangeable schemes of value.

Implicitly, then, disorder in one field of necessary harmony causes reflected disorder elsewhere. Disturbance in the marriage of Oberon and Titania causes disturbance in the world of nature, which serves and depends on them, and this in turn causes confusion and distress in the human world. This is the nearest that *A Midsummer Night's Dream* comes to the idea of the 'great chain of being', which finds its most powerful dramatic expression in the great tragedies. In *King Lear* there are violent natural storms which reflect the disturbance of human family relationships and hierarchies of authority, and there are inner mental disturbances which also reflect familial disorder through the onset of madness. In *Macbeth* the murder of a king is reflected in the physical universe (it remains dark all day and Duncan's horses, part of his obedient retinue in the right course of things, attack and eat each other) and in the individual mind (Lady Macbeth goes mad). In the world of comedy and fantasy which is *A Midsummer Night's Dream*, the consequences of unnatural disharmony are not so serious, prolonged and insistent, but they are essentially of the same kind. The breach between Oberon and Titania carries resonances of natural, climatic, procreative and ritualistic disorder which impinges on the human world, and the speech has thematic significance for the play as a whole. For a moment, the unities and disaffections of love take on a universal quality and stand revealed in their power to protect or harm. For a moment, too, we have a vivid, concrete yet perspective vision of nature and natural forces, as they interpenetrate the whole play through immediate and localized occurrences. The nature of nature is by rooted disposition orderly and benevolent, as Titania is; but it has a potential of capriciousness, confusion, even of malignity when its own essential balances are disturbed, a cosmic endorsement of what we meet in Oberon and Puck. For a moment, finally, we have a vision, as a privileged audience, of forces which are unrevealed to human characters in the play. When human intelligence, represented pre-eminently by

Theseus, attempts to elevate the rational and place all exper...
it, it does so in ignorance of the natural and cosmic forces
fairies represent and which Titania's great aria describes.

The musical reply within the play, the balancing vision of ...
harmony and order as the human mind perceives it when all is w..., is
the duet between Theseus and Hippolyta just before the discovery of the
sleeping lovers (IV.i.102–26). The royal couple have gone hunting, the
aftermath of their May Day rites of celebration, and Theseus gives order
for the hounds to be released. The pleasure they anticipate is not so
much the chase, but rather the music of the baying hounds. In the three
speeches of the duet there is a residue of former rivalry between these
lovers. Hippolyta harks back to earlier, pre-Theseus times in other
places, when she heard the Spartan hounds give tongue in wild, animal
music which, she is plainly hinting, the hounds of Theseus will do pretty
well to beat. Theseus takes up the challenge, arguing that his hounds are
bred from Spartan hounds and, we might guess, bred for improvement.
The hint of contest and rivalry, a rivalry set chiefly in the discordant past
rather than the harmonious present, only emphasizes the concord they
have achieved, a concord which can gently *play* with rivalry as the
affectionate left-over reminiscence of past fighting.

This human truth, of personal concord won from discord, underlies
the generalizing image in sound and vision which is the primary effect of
the duet. In the occasion itself, and in the memories it stirs, there is a
sudden opening of new vistas, partly of time but most importantly of
place. The hounds are to be uncoupled 'in the western valley', implicitly
at the opposite point of the compass from the easternness of sunrise
ritual. To hear them, Theseus and Hippolyta will ascend 'up to the
mountain's top'. Height and space are suddenly opened up from the
restrictive confines of the night-time wood. From this extended vicinity
of Athens we move out through Hippolyta's speech to 'a wood of Crete',
on a bear hunt with 'hounds of Sparta'. The play's vision of its imaginary
Greece now extends still further, and even in tiny details the central
concept of the speech is reinforced. Sparta was traditionally the enemy
of Athens, but Hercules (as we are reminded when Theseus is selecting
the evening's entertainment) is the Duke's kinsman. Hippolyta's
recollection mingles hints of concord within discord; when Theseus
replies, his suggestion of still greater concord extends the geographic
range yet further, to Thessaly.

The primary image of concord within discord lies, however, with the
hounds themselves, and appropriately with music. Again the cumulative
image is one of almost limitless extension. The hounds themselves make

music, 'matched in mouth like bells,/Each under each'. The natural servants of ducal authority conspire in choral tunefulness, and are appreciated (the opposite of the piping winds whom Oberon and Titania disregarded). From the mountain-top, Theseus and Hippolyta will hear not only the hounds, but 'hounds and echo in conjunction' – a musical reciprocation between animals and the containing landscape. Even this suggestion of expansive harmony, however, is outdone by Hippolyta's re-creation of remembered natural music:

> Never did I hear
> Such gallant chiding, for besides the groves,
> The skies, the fountains, every region near
> Seemed all one mutual cry.
>
> (IV.i.113–16)

Woodland, air and water all conjoin in a musical effect which spreads across space and recollected time to produce a contradictory and paradoxical harmony, 'So musical a discord, such sweet thunder'.

The richest single word in the duet, and the one of most significance for the play, is 'confusion'; in speaking of 'musical confusion', Theseus accepts the word 'confusion' with its suggestion of disorder, and superimposes on it the latinate precision of 'harmonious blending', flowing together, making two things one.

The disposition of ideas in the duet is a signal of the way such passages work in *A Midsummer Night's Dream*; some of the key ideas and phrases occur early, and the sequential nature of the speeches as character dialogue is subordinate to their total effect. The reciprocal voices of actor and actress must compete gently in their individual guises, but subordinate their rivalry to a pleased accord of vocal music.

We find the duet in its most artificial and conspicuous form in the exchange between Lysander and Hermia about the dangerous fatedness of love (I.i.132–49). While Lysander opens and closes the exchange, its centrepiece is a passage of single alternate lines where the lovers in turn pronounce and lament the external differences which threaten the inner mutuality of love. This is stichomythia, a rigid dialogue of alternate lines derived from Greek drama. Both the New Penguin Shakespeare editor, Stanley Wells, and the New Arden Shakespeare editor, Harold Brooks, aptly quote the observation of Bernard Shaw on these lines: 'Shakespeare makes the two star-crossed lovers speak in alternate lines with an effect which sets the whole scene throbbing with their absorption in one another', and Brooks cites his further comment, coming aptly from a fellow-dramatist, that 'with a Hermia who knows how to breathe out these parentheses the duet is an exquisite one' (Bernard Shaw, *Our Theatre in the Nineties* Vol. 1 (1932), p. 180). The hint is a good one, and accurately points to the libretto quality of the text. The passage is this:

LYSANDER	The course of true love never did run smooth;
	But either it was different in blood –
HERMIA	O cross! – too high to be enthralled to low.
LYSANDER	Or else misgraffèd in respect of years –
HERMIA	O spite! – too old to be engaged to young.
LYSANDER	Or else it stood upon the choice of friends –
HERMIA	O hell! – to choose love by another's eyes.
LYSANDER	Or if there were a sympathy in choice,
	War, death, or sickness did lay siege to it ...

(I.i.134–42)

In part Hermia is replying to Lysander, returning an emotional endorsement to his litany of complaint and thus reaffirming their own threatened union. As dialogue, the responses give scope for individual character; only the third misfortune threatens Hermia herself, and she could mark it by a sharpened intensity of feeling. But this, though actable, is really a misreading of the passage. Hermia's responses are delivered to herself at least as much as to Lysander, and, as Shaw proposes, they should be 'breathed out' almost as asides, a series of shocks, eased into choric generality by the fixed linguistic pattern. Rooted as it must be in the lovers' immediate crisis, the duet's formality extends it to a general lament for the universal hazards of young love.

While the hazards concern the binding of one to another in compulsory mismatching, the duet of mutual lovers is sustained. As soon as Lysander turns to the external and impersonal destructors which assail those like himself and Hermia who agree in loving, the duet becomes an aria, and an important one. It introduces key terms for the individual love-plights of the comedy – 'momentany', 'shadow', 'dream', 'night', 'darkness', 'confusion' – but with such reflective lyric sorrow that it becomes the play's generalized diagnosis of endangered love. Its resonances remain, a distantly audible statement with its poignancy remembered, to offset the comic and synthetic dangers of the love plot.

The play gives weight to its serious moments, but also keeps them in check by tactical reductiveness and parody. Only some fifty lines later (I.i.194–200) there is another duet of alternating lines, this time between Helena and Hermia, but with no such serious effect. The exchange has its formal tennis-rally of antitheses, but here they underscore the artificial opposites and similarities which give the lovers' plot its dancelike symmetry. And eventually, just as so many chickens come home to roost in the mechanicals' interlude, this formal single-line duet is no exception, reaching its farcical downfall in the duet between Pyramus and Thisbe at the wall's chink.

In general, however, the arias and duets are the play's imaginative excursions beyond Athens and the wood into the world, and beyond the localized tribulations of comic figures into the broader and more distant landscapes of human occupation and experience. They generalize the play, and locate its comedy within a framework of ideas.

Theseus and Hippolyta

We have looked already at two duets between Theseus and Hippolyta: the opening lines of the play and the Act IV passage about the music of the hounds. In each case there is an element of contradiction, argument and counter-argument, or rivalry, implicit in the lines; in each case it is overlaid by the mutuality of their expectation and pleasure; and in each case the duet has a thematic weight which takes it outside the confines of individual characterization.

Considerations of this kind affect the playing of Theseus and Hippolyta throughout the play. All the time we have a balance to maintain between their interest as people and their importance as structural presences or thematic voices. They are important because of who they are, but arguably more important still for *what* they are and *where* they are. In reading and guiding the playing of the two roles, the director's task is to combine the couple's formal complementary doubleness (as evident for instance in the two duets) and their 'realistic' individuation.

There is some scope for suggesting that all is not entirely well between these two. The traces of antagonism or competition we have noted in the duet speeches can be exploited by the director, together with the hints of earlier love affairs and infidelities on the part of both and the fact that their betrothal's origin lies in war and conquest, to suggest that this is really an enforced, reluctant marriage on Hippolyta's part and a trophy of victory on the part of Theseus. Silences are important; the play's choreographic opportunities lie as much in things unsaid as they do in speeches, and Hippolyta is entirely silent in Act I after her contribution to the first exchange. This has allowed the scene to be played with Hippolyta first using contradictory politeness as the weapon of subdued resentment, and then lapsing into watchful taciturnity for the rest of the scene. Theseus, on this reading, is much too busy sorting out Egeus and the rebellious lovers to take any further notice of her until his abrupt recollection of her presence at line 122: 'Come, my Hippolyta. What cheer, my love?' By thus exploiting every hint of suppressed antagonism, it is quite possible to sustain an anti-romantic or a feminist reading for the duration of the play.

To do this, however, involves disregarding the patterned nature of the play and the 'geometric' relationship of Theseus and Hippolyta to other groups of characters. If we place the stress, contrarily, on more formal significances, it is not necessary to forget realistic 'character' altogether. In the opening scene it is perfectly feasible that Hippolyta is silently opposed to the repressive legalistic treatment being meted out to Hermia. If she herself has won love and imminent marriage out of war, it would not be surprising if the arbitrary victimization of love in the case of another woman were to excite her compassion. There will be evidence in Act V of Hippolyta's capacity for generous compunction, and the actress would have no difficulty in silently conveying it here; if so, then Theseus' 'What cheer, my love?' would be the sudden recognition, on the part of one who for several minutes has been understandably distracted by noisy family quarrels, that his wife-to-be is upset.

Even if we take behavioural realism thus far, it is not necessary to take it still further and suppose that, when Theseus changes his mind about Hermia in Act IV and overrules Egeus, it is because Hippolyta has been at him in the meantime. I have seen highly unconvincing efforts to suggest this, by showing us a prompting and goading Hippolyta, after the lovers have been discovered, urging the Duke to do the gentlemanly and romantic thing.

Gentlemanly Theseus customarily is; romantic, on the whole, he is not. Except for certain interventions in the mechanicals' interlude, his speech is measured, serious and judicial. However, its authority and austerity are mitigated by benevolent and generous warmth, so he is quite capable of acting autonomously as a liberal court of appeal against the strict legal severities of Athenian judgement. Certainly there is a difference between the cool pronouncements of Act I:

> ... the law of Athens yields you up –
> Which by no means we may extenuate –
> To death or to a vow of single life.
> (I.i.119–21)

and the Act IV utterance of the very extenuation he has here refused: 'Egeus, I will overbear your will.' However, his first pronunciation of

Athenian law is in itself extenuation of the strict penalty first demanded by Egeus: Hermia's father did not offer the reprieve of lifelong chastity. Moreover, if Hippolyta is imagined as silently pitying Hermia's ordeal from the vantage point of her own premarital happiness, Theseus is gently voicing the same values of legitimate sexual joy through the tone of reverent distaste which he attaches to his portrait of a barren nun. The speech and silence of Theseus and Hippolyta in this first scene allow the possibility of union within hinted divergence that we find in the duets. Individuation of the two carries the dramatic interest of residual antagonisms, while their representative positions anticipate harmonious unity.

To say that Theseus is not, in general, romantic is clearly in need of support if indeed he promotes sexual fulfilment (or marital chastity) over singleness and abstention, and if he makes the law recognizant of love. Considered as an individual character, Theseus wants others to share his own impatiently anticipated joy; marriage stemming from love is delightfully infectious in his Athens. Considered as a representative figure of urban and rational authority, he personifies an order of things which celebrates the appropriate expression of natural instinct. There is still, however, a due emphasis upon legitimacy: the final permitted disposition of alliances is not between those who are 'different in blood', and would not be allowed if it were. Theseus stands for the rationality of social law, but within its due constraints he enfranchises the private impulses of love.

This makes of Theseus a most impressive order-figure in the play. The 'framing' world of Athens is most intelligently, generously and courteously governed. He combines a number of formal roles: governor, judge, mediator, patron, chief celebrant of May Day and the rites of marriage feasting, and in effect master of ceremonies at his own, eventually multiple, wedding (Philostrate is the agent, Theseus is the initiator). In all these roles he is the benevolent offstage protector of those entangled in anarchic comedy. The measured, dignified blank verse, on occasion neatly concluded by a rhyming couplet, is Shakespeare's chosen instrument to voice his gravitas and intellectual certainty. He also stands as the voice of 'cool reason', and it is here that his adequacy as a 'framing' figure, though essential to the play's implied design for human happiness, is shown to be limited. And it is here too that the complementary 'prompting' voice of Hippolyta, occasional though it is, provides a confirmatory human reservation to support our own privileged familiarity with the unsuspected fairy world.

Theseus' famous aria on the imagination, his 'the lunatic, the lover and the poet' speech, comes at the beginning of Act V, when all the wanderers are safely restored to the rational order of Athens. Considered as an aria, the speech has enormous thematic importance. The speaker's own lyric eloquence engenders a language which subverts his scepticism and provides a major statement of the play's key oppositions: between reason and madness, between reason and love, between reason and imagination. Lunatic, lover and poet are alike guilty of transformative imagination and hence, by implication, of generating illusions devoid of substance and truth. A major conceptual antithesis of the speech is between apprehension and comprehension, which can be best considered as a definitive distinction between primary perception and rational inference. Elsewhere we shall look at the place of this conceptual distinction in the intellectual vocabulary of the whole play, and ask whether it is adequate (see pp. 124–9). What matters here is that it is Theseus' way of defining; more than anything else, this speech gives the Duke his intellectual identity and limits. In a play dominated by eyes, Theseus names all his deluded imaginers as being misled by deceitful sight. The madman 'sees more devils than vast hell can hold'; the lover 'sees Helen's beauty in a brow of Egypt'; and the poet's eye rolls in frenzy. But Theseus is untrue to his own doctrine of logical rationalism, because the fantasies that beget these delusory visions are themselves shaping, and 'the poet's pen/Turns them to shapes'. The Duke is, in fact, undecided whether his dismissive inadvertent eulogy is resting on the notion of misinterpreted sensory data or on visual embodiments of internally generated nothings.

Hippolyta is again the contradictory, complementary voice. For Theseus the question is: Are these things true? For Hippolyta the statement is: These things are strange. To his analytical reason she counterposes a readiness to entertain the prospect of mystery.

Viewing them as realistic characters, we find evidence of unthreatening but lively disagreement. Both as people and as figures in the pattern, we find the discrepancy taking a certain regularity of form; that is, Hippolyta's mind is more venturesome, somewhat freer in time and space, more imaginative (or simply more credulous) than that of Theseus. Up to the beginning of Act V, the effect of her occasional contributions is enlarging; it has a personal quality similar to that of the arias, in opening up extended vistas of possibility beyond the generous but rationally contained domain of Theseus. Yet the complementarity rather than competition of the two is affirmed by their shared music, the grave and measured blank verse which can take off at one word's notice into lyric celebration.

Because this is the established pattern until the court is foregathered for the mechanicals' play, it is all the more interesting that in this last appearance their complementary roles should suddenly be reversed (see pp. 138–40).

The lovers

The character, or lack of it, of the four lovers, and the nature of the language Shakespeare gives them, have always provoked much critical discontent. Their poetic romanticism of speech is accused of being 'artificial', not in the neutral or indeed complimentary sense which it carries in this study, but as a term of abuse. The style is found to be flaccid, cliché-ridden, gestural and emptily rhetorical, self-consciously poetic, predictably formal and trite in its usual dependence on the rhyming couplet. The characters are likewise written off as cardboard figures, lacking in individuality, the men virtually indistinguishable from each other and the women separated only by a very obvious, crude difference of colouring and height.

Defenders of the play have often been at pains to refute these accusations by finding some differences at whatever cost, impelled (one suspects) by the conviction that because this is Shakespeare such differences are certain to exist. An excellent example of this effort is cited by Antony W. Price in his *Casebook* collection of criticism, from the nineteenth-century critic H. Woelffel:

> If we gather, as it were, into one focus all the separate, distinguishing traits of [Lysander and Demetrius], if we seek to read the secret of their nature in their eyes, we shall unquestionably find it to be this, viz. in Lysander the poet wished to represent a noble magnanimous nature sensitive to the charms of the loveliness of soul and of spiritual beauty; but in Demetrius he has given us a nature fundamentally less noble; in its final analysis, even unlovely, and sensitive only to the impression of physical beauty.
>
> (*Casebook*, p. 35)

What is noticeable about this confident attempt to differentiate the two is that its contrivance falls into just that pattern of balance and opposition which is characteristic of the play. Woelffel has not really individualized the characters, but distinguished them within a geometric framework: Lysander loves internal beauty, Demetrius loves external beauty. The play's formal structures seem to defeat all effort to evade them.

Within very modest limits, it is in fact quite possible to separate the lovers, at least well enough to give actors and actresses some purchase on their individual roles. The difference between Helena and Hermia is psychological as well as physical. Hermia's speech to Theseus in the first scene is not 'pert', as was suggested by one critic who clearly felt that the young should be kept in their place, but it *is* politely firm and determined, and she maintains this positive, self-assertive role throughout. When need be, it can intensify to sheer aggression, as it does when she is unexpectedly put at disadvantage by Helena and threatens to attack her eyes. Physical restraint is needed to cope with Hermia when her blood is up: 'though she be but little, she is fierce'. No such curbing measures would be needed with the gentle Helena, who is physically much larger than Hermia, but a very maiden for her cowardice. Their languages of anguished protest are similarly characterized; Hermia spits vituperation, while Helena prefers a plaintive, ironic, and rhetorically self-addressed remonstrance. The very direction of their speeches when they are up against it – instinctively outward-turning on Hermia's part, inward-turning on Helena's – reflects their relative positions within the quartet. Hermia is customarily at its actively socialized centre and quickly reasserts her place there even when excluded, whilst Helena is always relatively isolated, a fringe figure, retaining some of that solitary placement which she took in Athens in the opening scene. At the level of traceable individuation these tendencies exist alongside the dominant movement of the play, which places the two women in symmetrical and equalized positions in the love dance.

Lysander and Demetrius are harder to separate, but the difference noted by Woelffel has an element of truth. In the opening scene the situations of the two men are different, even though their speeches are very similar and much stress is placed on their social equality; Lysander is already locked into the privacy of a love relationship, while Demetrius is referring his claims to the public nature of Athenian citizenship. Demetrius exacts a political imprimatur for his claim to Hermia, Lysander an emotional one. Residual traces of this circumstantial difference are carried over to the woodland scenes. For example, a rude colloquial dismissiveness towards unwanted females comes more naturally to Demetrius. There is something histrionic, not to say inelegantly helpless, about Lysander's efforts to shake off Hermia ('Out, loathèd medicine!/O hated potion, hence!'), while Demetrius performing the same role towards Helena displays a terse and charmless candour ('For I am sick when I do look on thee'). Speech for speech, Demetrius seems a slightly less poetic figure. He has, so to speak, travelled slightly less far from Athens than Lysander, and this is a marginal difference compatible with their respective states of urban social orthodoxy.

Even so, discoverable differences *are* marginal. There is enough to give the actor or actress a graspable identity, but no more. By far the greatest emphasis is on their similarity, and the most important divergences we can find between them are thematic in significance rather than contributing to meaningful difference of character. Elsewhere we have examined the dancelike patterning of the lovers' scenes, and the insulated, playlike quality of their activities as a foursome in the wood. In the following discussion I shall try to show how their characteristic language reinforces these effects, often interacting with the physicality of their actions and supplying choreographic indicators for it.

When Helena and Demetrius appear in the wood for the second time, their brief dialogue is a miniature duet of imploring and rejecting, meeting and parting, opening and closing of physical space. The lines prescribe the pulsating movement of the action:

HELENA   Stay though thou kill me, sweet Demetrius!
DEMETRIUS   I charge thee hence; and do not haunt me thus.
HELENA   O, wilt thou darkling leave me? Do not so!
DEMETRIUS   Stay, on thy peril. I alone will go.

                                             (II.ii.90–93)

The closed form of the couplet technically counteracts the ostensible meaning of the lines. Demetrius, in accepting the pattern of audible rhythmic completions, is so to speak participating linguistically with Helena in constructing their quarrel; verse artifice reduces meaning to convention, and confines discord within a predetermined pattern. The exchange of antithesis (stay/hence/leave/go) confirms the countering sharedness of the dialogue and offsets its rancorous hostility. The movements required give the same impression of double or contrary impulse; they involve the players in moving toward and away from each other. It would be a very wooden and unphysical production which asked the actors to stand still and face each other for these lines; their instructions for approach and recoil are contained in simple details of the language. This is typical of the lovers' speeches, where apparently thin, formal and declamatory verbal gesture contains more than it may seem to.

Included in the first hostile passage of the woodland scenes is the association between love and death, something which Helena had already announced at the end of Act II scene i as the funereal desire contained in her passion for Demetrius:

> I'll follow thee, and make a heaven of hell,
> To die upon the hand I love so well
>
> (II.i.243–4)

and which she repeats at III.ii.244, when she thinks herself the victim of jeering scorn. These gloomy expectations are directed at Demetrius, who has indeed made some unconvincing threats of violence against his unwanted lover. In her turn, Hermia suspects Demetrius of having killed Lysander (III.ii.56). They both link Demetrius with violence. Lysander, on the other hand, when he is accused by Demetrius of cowardice in pretending that Hermia is physically restraining him from duelling, protests:

> What? Should I hurt her, strike her, kill her dead?
> Although I hate her, I'll not harm her so.
>
> (III.ii.269–70)

There is some pretext here for further differentiation of character: a violent, unchivalrous Demetrius, a gentle and more courteous Lysander. These are trace elements of realism existing within a dominant artifice. In truth there is no death threat to these figures, and we know it. The lovers are decorating their maverick absurdities with extravagant claims to serious mortality. Their language does not reinforce their seriousness, but undermines it. A comic convention here neutralizes love's potential for tragedy, not so farcically but just as certainly as it will later do in 'Pyramus and Thisbe'; in both cases the counteractive effect of comic security is achieved by the combined effect of dramatic language and performance styles. Appropriate to their two environments (and two levels of audience distance from the action), these scenes form a very controlled and safe reminder, delivered under the protection of declared theatrical unrealism, that love and death can indeed be close companions.

If the lovers' scenes comprise a muted and less publicly theatrical version of the mechanicals' play of doomed love, they also incorporate a quieter and subtler version of the audience-on-stage. Considering the lovers as 'characters', we found that Helena's position is the odd one out. Even when *formally* inseparable from the quartet movement (as she always is), she is the one who feels victimized by and alienated from the romantic confederacy of the others. In this role she behaves as if she were an audience (albeit a targeted and vulnerable one). During the confusions following Puck's mistake, and the first stage of its correction, she believes that the other three have ganged up to mock her. Several times she speaks to herself as if they had put on a cruel play for her especial torment, and protest at her ill-treatment is mingled with comic comment on performance. When Lysander declares 'My love, my life, my soul, fair Helena!', his romantic hyperbole is put in its place by Helena's 'O, excellent!', while Hermia's vitriolic anger is met with 'Fine, i'faith'. Like the more obviously participant audience of Act V, Helena's embroiled spectatorship is the live audience's cue to recognize the scene's theatrical artifice.

The woodland scenes typically overstate their own theatricality; this is an essential part of their method. At its most blatant we can see this process at the dividing lines between sleep and waking. Human beings go to sleep when tired, yet this most natural of bodily processes becomes artificial in the lovers' wood. The natural harmony of lovers falling asleep is rendered artificial for Lysander and Hermia (II.ii.71) because of their strange surroundings, their chastely separate encampments, and their synchronized dropping off. At III.ii.87, Demetrius' abandoned chasing of Hermia and opting for sleep is made contrived by its abruptness. This staging of synthetic naturalness is far exceeded, of course, by the artifice of waking. At II.ii.109, Lysander, stirred by the anxious Helena, leaps up to instantaneous ardent wakefulness with 'And run through fire I will for thy sweet sake!' The love juice has done its work, and its work is utterly to abolish the conscious interval between one romantic loyalty and another. At III.ii.137, Demetrius undergoes the same experience, its extravagant comic suddenness underscored by Lysander's preceding line, 'Demetrius loves her, and he loves not you.' For Demetrius too, the change of love is marked by exaggerated articulacy the moment his eyes are open: 'O Helen, goddess, nymph, perfect, divine . . .'

Theatrical and linguistic means are used with deliberate and self-advertising over-emphasis to serve a thematic end. Each of these events, both falling asleep and waking, are staged examples of the theatre cue. The convenient event or spoken word provokes a reaction which is comic in its over-neatness; the timing is absurdly over-perfect. Everything happens in accord with rhythmic plot contrivance, so completely as it should that it should not! In this lies the protective comedy which has spare accommodation for distress.

Not only is the artifice of the lovers' scenes thus guarded and proclaimed, but, more importantly still, the lovers and their inadvertent play are integrated with the drama's central themes: the irrationality of love, the confusingness of premarital allegiance and its instability, the brevity of love ('brief as the lightning in the collied night'), the virtual simultaneity of opposites, the mystery of sleep and dream and night, and above all the experience of transformation. The play's most serious themes are presented in the lovers' play under the comic protection of histrionic excess.

Certain of these themes are embedded in the very nature of the lovers' language. The trouble with them is not that they are foolish, but that they are intelligent people in an inherently foolish situation. They are citizens of Theseus' Athens, suddenly entangled in the incomprehensible wood. In the terms which Theseus will employ in Act V, they apprehend much but comprehend nothing. Reason will not avail them in the effort to understand the experience of irrational love. Even so, the language they habitually use is not at all irrational or foolish, except at moments when the pressure of behavioural absurdities has driven them to violent reactions. The comedy of language represented by the lovers is that of attempted rationality where reason is inadequate.

Much of the stiltedness and unconvincingness of the lovers' speeches derives from mistaken efforts to apply the processes of reason. Critics who complain that Shakespeare is writing badly in these scenes are overlooking the simple truth that inadequate language is often dramatically necessary. There are several stylistic habits of the lovers which powerfully express the incongruous *mental* habits of urbane Athenian youth. When Helena is remonstrating with Lysander because he has suddenly deserted Hermia for herself in what she takes to be erratic, superficial dotage, she protests:

> These vows are Hermia's. Will you give her o'er?
> Weigh oath with oath, and you will nothing weigh.
> Your vows to her and me, put in two scales,
> Will even weigh, and both as light as tales.
>
> (III.ii.130–33)

Underlying the satiric comedy of these lines is Shakespeare's dramatized amusement with the hackneyed poetic devices of courtly verse in the period. Why is there a tautology here, the poetic amplification of the last two lines adding nothing either to Helena's argumentative protest or to the metaphor she has chosen? Amplification without development is the rhetorical effect of the lines. A Helena genuinely moved by accusatory emotion would not speak in this way. What she really does is to display satisfaction with the foolproof nature of her metaphor for use argument; she has found a trim way of saying that contradictory in oaths cancel each other out. The argument is a fair one, but so satisfactory that she cannot resist repeating it. Metaphor-as-argument, the sophisticated rhetoric of youthful Athens, is overriding emotion, and the supposedly outraged Helena takes pleasure in bringing it under the tutelage of reason and wit to demonstrate a proof.

The exchange which follows confirms the process, and introduces into the debate (for this is essentially what it is) one of the key terms of the play:

LYSANDER   I had no judgement when to her I swore.
HELENA   Nor none in my mind now you give her o'er.
                         (III.ii.134–5)

This, however, is the Helena who declared, even before the woodland tribulations started, 'Nor hath love's mind of any judgement taste' (I.i.236). Despite such passages of reflection, especially when they are uttered in the intellectual shelter of rational Athens, the habit of appeal to reason and judgement is irresistible, especially in self-defence against the confusions of the wood. The comedy of the lovers and their speech lies largely in the fact that the further they are removed from circumstances where reason holds sway, the more frequently they try to appeal to it. 'Judgement' – as he normally understands the term – has nothing whatever to do with Lysander's change of fealty, and Helena, by her own memorable earlier protestation, is well placed to tell him so; instead, she accepts his terms and responds accordingly.

Such habits of desperate rationality are spread stylistically across the lovers' speeches. They are apparent in their fondness for half-lines and split-line structures, allowing epigrammatic balance and antithesis within a single line unit and hence a simple economy of contrastive argument. In the most emotive situations they fall for the temptations of inappropriate wit.

The balanced couplet, the second line neatly contradicting the first, is an even more frequent habit of expression, and again it should perhaps be noticed that Helena, in human terms the outsider, is the most compulsive and effective stylist of them all. Again an example may illustrate the point:

> To vow, and swear, and superpraise my parts,
> When, I am sure, you hate me with your hearts.
> You both are rivals, and love Hermia:
> And now both rivals to mock Helena.
>   (III.ii.153–6)

These lines are spoken by a Helena in crisis – she has just been knocked sideways by the overblown renaissance of Demetrius' devotion – yet these lines indicate no forfeiture of intellectual control; the cogent rationality of antithesis is still in charge of her speech. In four lines she contrasts outward protestation and inward truth; external and internal bodily realities: praise and mockery; love and hate; herself and Hermia; and two contrasting rivalries. Moreover, the immediate personal exchange illuminates a major dramatic theme. Ruth Nevo has drawn attention to the play's motif of rivalry (see *Comic Transformations in Shakespeare*, p. 100), and this passage brings it to the forefront in the context of a neatly balanced statement. This is not the language of a character in distress, overcome by the perplexity of individual torment, but it *is* the language of someone whose confident linguistic precision is unequal to the situation in which she finds herself. She is well able to understand Lysander and Demetrius as maliciously conspiring reasoning creatures (which they are not), but hopelessly unable to understand them as competitive and genuinely devoted lovers in the grip of irrational passion (which they are). The shared movement of the quartet's dream is complemented by the shared rationalism which they unsuccessfully use to control it, and the language is skilfully devised to fit.

Other such stylistic habits are redundant repetition, not, as with Helena's example above, for the purpose of reiterated proof, but simply as formal gesturing (language equivalent to slapping the table for emphasis); finicky subdivisions of phrasing and meaning (the equivalent of 'let me leave no possible scope for misunderstanding'); and artificial switches between literal and metaphoric usage. An example of redundant repetition can be found in Demetrius' overblown compliment to Helena, quoted earlier, when he wakes up to his new passion: 'O Helen, goddess, nymph, perfect, divine' (III.ii.137). This overdone stockpiling of worshipful epithets has grown still further when Helena hurls it back in protest later in the scene – so much so that it overspills a line:

> To call me goddess, nymph, divine and rare,
> Precious, celestial . . .
>
> (III.ii.226–7)

Accumulating words which scarcely differ in meaning, Demetrius expresses ludicrous adoration and Helena a bitterly ironic complaint.

An ingenious subdivision of meaning, characteristic of the lovers, occurs in Hermia's meditation on sight and hearing when she finds her lost Lysander:

> Dark night that from the eye his function takes
> The ear more quick of apprehension makes.
> Wherein it doth impair the seeing sense
> It pays the hearing double recompense.
>
> (III.ii.177–80)

These two pairs of lines are not quite identical in meaning. In the second couplet Hermia is refining her point by suggesting that the ear gains sensitivity to precisely the same degree as the eye loses it. She elaborates her point (and in the process makes it absurd) by claiming for it an exact and mathematical equivalence.

The habit of switching between literal and metaphoric usage is exemplified by Hermia's speech to Demetrius at III.ii.65–73. Demetrius' surly plans for the hypothetical corpse of Lysander ('I had rather give his carcass to my hounds') are countered by Hermia with an abusive metaphoric seizure of his statement ('Out, dog! Out, cur!'), and a few lines later she repeats the whole process for herself, first thinking of Lysander stung by a genuine adder and then exploiting the idea as a suitable impromptu metaphor for Demetrius. A casual rhetoric of associationism permits the lovers to move with spontaneous ease between the literal and the metaphoric for the sake of argument.

What these stylistic habits have in common is their purpose of imposing rationality and intelligibility upon the chaos of experience, in a world of night and dream where fantasy and imagination are at large, love is disobedient to reason, and apprehension rather than comprehension is the ruling order of perception. Their language *needs* to be ineffective, but that is not because they are fools; it is because they are too clever for their own good, in the wrong place. On the part of critics, impatient misreadings of these scenes can readily stem from the over-generalized valuing of rational intelligence which is, ironically, the lovers' own mistake. The passage of central thematic importance in this connection is Lysander's, and in speaking it he is, by the play's own terms of reference, intelligent, rational, and absurdly misinformed:

> The will of man is by his reason swayed,
> And reason says you are the worthier maid.
> Things growing are not ripe until their season;
> So I, being young, till now ripe not to reason.
> And touching now the point of human skill,
> Reason becomes the marshal to my will . . .
>
> (II.ii.121–6)

Lysander is not misinformed on the grounds that reason has no place at all in the conduct of love and its eventuality of marriage, but because it has no place in the particular occasion of love's choice. Here as elsewhere the play creates but disqualifies a false antithesis between reason and sight, between rational and sensory data, intellectual and visual truth. There are cunning false trails in the text of just this kind, and one is offered here in Lysander's next line, when he declares that reason 'leads me to your eyes'. Confusion between eyes as perceivers and eyes as objects of beauty perceived acts as a (deliberate?) red herring in the play. The true antithesis is between inner forces for which sight is the mediator – between reason and imagination, or between reason and the potent instincts which lie always on the edge of knowledge and understanding, yet determine the 'irrational' progress of love and hate. This inner dualism is magnificently represented in external form by the complementary monarchies of Athens and the wood, of day and night. The lovers' shared error, which governs the verbal comedy of their scenes, is their disastrous effort to interpret these other forces by the language of reason, or, in other words, to interpret the wood by Athens. Not for nothing are their speeches characterized by miniature exercises in logical reasoning, and by metaphor functioning as argument.

C. L. Barber notes of those scenes that 'The farce is funniest, and most meaningful, in the climactic scene where the lovers are most unwilling, where they try their hardest to use personality to break free, and still are willy-nilly swept along to end in pitch darkness, trying to fight.' This is fairly said, but needs the extra qualification that their most strenuous efforts to enlist personality in the struggle for freedom take the form of reasoned passion, emotion dressed in argument.

An example of this which has major thematic significance for the play is Helena's appeal to Hermia to abandon her apparent treachery and conspiracy with the men, on the basis of their childhood friendship. In support of her plea she recalls their idyllic girlhood, and the innocence it held for them. This speech (III.ii.192–219) is of the highest importance for the play as a whole. The children were, significantly, 'like two artificial gods'. Helena's celebration of this childhood deity is marked by a long succession of linked images, each of them deriving its force from the concept of *two as one*. The children jointly, or doubly as if singly, embroidered the same flower on the same sampler, they sat on the same cushion and – importantly again in a play where music is the prime image of harmony and peace – they sang the same song in the same key.

91

Helena then intensifies this image of oneness. It begins with sharing but becomes 'incorporation', an interpenetration of bodies, with a common root and vital organs common to them both.

The argument is both mathematical and attractive, but it is flawed. Barber notes its imperfection: 'Before the scramble is over, the two girls have broken the double-cherry bond, to fight each without reserve for her man. So they move from the loyalties of one stage of life to those of another' (*Shakespeare's Festive Comedy*, p. 130). This important idea remained with Shakespeare and resurfaced in a far more serious form many years later, in *The Winter's Tale*. At the beginning of that play Polixenes, King of Bohemia, is paying a state visit to Leontes, King of Sicilia. The two were brought up together, but each is now married, with a son of his own. Leontes' queen, Hermione, asks Polixenes to tell her about their childhood, and he answers:

> We were as twinned lambs that did frisk i'th'sun
> And bleat the one at th'other. What we changed
> Was innocence for innocence: we knew not
> The doctrine of ill-doing, nor dreamed
> That any did.
>
> (*The Winter's Tale*, I.ii.67–71)

In this same scene Leontes is overcome by an apparently sudden and irrational fit of sexual jealousy, wrongly suspecting Hermione and Polixenes of adultery. In truth his jealousy seems explicable only if we see it as directed not against people but against time. Reminded of idyllic childhood, he is suddenly unable to come to terms with the loss and change that come with adult sexuality, and the usurpation of childhood innocence by his own child; he cannot accept the transition from one stage or condition of life to another. The language itself in Polixenes' idealized recall is inflammatory. Although there is no such psychological explosion in the conventional world of *A Midsummer Night's Dream*, we can nevertheless see that the grounds of Helena's reproof to Hermia are much the same. She remembers their youth, their monosexual twinning, their absorption in childhood activities, and their innocence, just as Polixenes does; and, like an ingenuous prototype of Leontes, she sees in her childhood twin an act of sexual treachery, taking the form of a conspiracy with the opposite sex designed to humiliate her. The very terms of her remonstrance (''tis not maidenly') involve denying that they have been overtaken by the natural sequence of sexual transitions, in this case from childhood sexual innocence to the changed priorities and loyalties of courtship. For her the obsolete intimacy of childhood expresses itself in recall of physical identification, even though the record of her appearances in the play is marked by pained awareness of their physical difference and sexual rivalry. The mathematical and cerebral formula of two persons idealistically becoming one is the rational centre of her protest, summarized in the crucial phrase that they achieved a 'union in partition'.

Lysander has earlier tried exactly the same argument on Hermia, for different purposes, at a different stage of the sexual cycle. When he and Hermia have arrived exhausted in the wood (Act II scene ii), they settle down to sleep, but not without some dispute as to where. Hermia is insistent that they are not married yet and that proprieties must be observed. She wants him at a safe distance, and uses the emphatic, oppositional, split-line formula to tell him so ('Lie further off yet; do not lie so near'). Like so many lines in the lovers' scenes, this instruction combines stylized artifice with individualizing opportunities of stress and movement for the actress. Lysander, however, has an argument ready to hand, and it is Helena's:

> One turf shall serve as pillow for us both;
> One heart, one bed, two bosoms, and one troth.
>
> (II.ii.47–8)

Like Helena he conscripts external objects to his argumentative convenience; the single turf does just as well as the single sampler when you need additional persuasive oneness. Bodily dualism is undeniable and, anyway, important: a twinning partnership is the rationale of both enterprises. Lysander uses the phrase 'two bosoms' three times, but (exactly as with Helena's biological metaphor of 'two seeming bodies but one heart') Lysander takes advantage of the heart's singleness and develops the idea with just the amused, logical, seductive wit of a metaphysical poet:

> I mean that my heart unto yours is knit,
> So that but one heart we can make of it.
>
> (II.ii.53–4)

Even the appeal to innocence is shared with Helena's persuasive methods.

The cumulative effect is one of common ground. The quartet of lovers share a vocabulary of verbal and intellectual artifice. They all know the rules of the game. Hermia appreciates Lysander's performance even when she refutes it ('Lysander riddles very prettily'). Language is dancing in set figures which are consciously understood, even while the lovers' actions are a dance controlled by others, whose ethereal existence they do not suspect. The linguistic comedy of the lovers derives from their known Athenian world, while their situational comedy derives from the unfamiliar and perplexing wood. At times they can play their language games safely, as Lysander and Hermia do here, because the wood is not at that point impinging on them. The greater their embroilment in the wood's disorder, the greater their linguistic insufficiency, and the sharper the comedy of their efforts to depend on it.

In Hermia's gentle fending off of her companion, a further term is introduced: 'But, gentle friend, for love and *courtesy*/Lie further off'. Like so many of the central thematic ideas in the lovers' scenes, this one is mainly entrusted to Helena, in practice. Discussion of these scenes often neglects it, concentrating exclusively on the language of romantic love. As a positive and negative feature of the lovers' transactions, it is in fact conspicuous. Helena protests to her supposed tormentors:

> If you were civil and knew courtesy
> You would not do me thus much injury.
> (III.ii.147–8)

and later tells the others that they would not treat her so scornfully if they had 'any pity, grace, or manners'. Strong as the positive ideal may be, the vocabulary of its omission is still stronger. Helena's vocabulary is weighted in her 'ordeal' with the language of extreme discourtesy: 'scorn', 'mockery', 'derision', 'flout', 'disdain', 'abuse', 'bait', 'spurn', 'despise'.

Here in fact is a separate though correlative instance of disturbance in the natural order of things. During their love trials, the lovers generate extremes of discourtesy which offend both the world they have come from and the world they have entered. Courtesy is not only an Athenian quality, exemplified in Theseus; it is also a part of the wood's right ordering of things when it is working well. The ground of Oberon's intervention, his reason for being offended with Demetrius, is not only his failure to reciprocate Helena's love, but his disdainfulness. In Titania's speech about the seasonal disorders we saw the cosmic churlishness which echoed the disorder between the fairy couple. Courtesy takes its place among the play's selective patterning of order and disorder. Important as it is for Hermia and Helena, it has echoes in occasions elsewhere in the wood, and is carried forward to the clarifying action of Act V.

It remains to notice the impressive change in the lovers' diction when (at IV.i.138) they awaken to the woodland morning and the presence of Theseus. The habitual couplets change to blank verse; the witty argumentative metaphors become similes, attempting to explain themselves to themselves; and so much emphasis on 'troth' becomes a single truthfulness. The sign of their progression is that they take on dignity while seeming to surrender it. The end of this scene is marked both by a new surprised composure in their waking roles and by a residual strandedness in the half-world between full consciousness and dream. There has, as we know, been one dream within the 'dream': Hermia's is vividly described. There have been sleeps within a whole now understood by them as sleep; Oberon's promise is fulfilled, that they will recall only 'the fierce vexation of a dream'. But, except for its internal sleeps and Hermia's dream, the audience knows that this is *not* a dream. The short passage of shared, quiet mystification (IV.i.186–98), is deeply relevant to the drama's total meaning, above all in its dualism. The artificialities of 'two as one' are genuine now. Hermia sees 'with parted eye/When everything seems double', Helena's new-found Demetrius is 'mine own and not mine own', Demetrius himself is perhaps awake, and 'yet we sleep, we dream'. For a moment, held between worlds, apprehension of doubleness becomes almost comprehension, even for the characters; the audience is better placed to know the truth and make it lasting.

If childhood was for Helena a rationalizing image of 'two as one', if Lysander's corresponding image was a premature and 'innocent' seduction, its true expression is approaching in the form of marriage, where 'These couples shall eternally be knit'. The transition through life's stages is here approaching its celebratory climax, gathering, in the process, rich extensions of its central concept of doubleness. Before that last phase, however, we need to look at parallel excursions through the wood, where echoes of these lovers' trials are audible in the very different voice of Bully Bottom.

Bottom and the mechanicals

Peter Quince's troupe of players is a wonderful example of the Elizabethan amateur companies, high in ambition and execrable in performance, cherishing hopes of turning professional in the years preceding Shakespeare's own career. The choicest moments for this group occur for all but Bottom in the interlude itself, which we shall look at separately. In their own persons they are authentic Warwickshire artisans, their roots many fathoms deep in England. Apart from Bottom and Quince there is little to individualize them. We know that Snug is 'slow of study' and probably best fitted with a roar-on part as the lion, and we know that Starveling can get quite effectively fed up with the interruptions of his ducal audience. We know that as a group they are fearful of causing offence by the terrifying realism of their performance. And that is really that.

'Nay, you must name his name,' says Bottom, and his advice is heeded wonderfully well. There is a lovingness for names in the mechanicals' scenes. The roll-call of actors in Act I scene ii is an excuse to name names that they all know perfectly well, and as often as possible they are said in full. The troupe is named by the name of its professions, too; Snug is additionally Snug because he is Snug the Joiner. A whole stratum of Elizabethan society is here, in the safe and certain knowledge of its place in the community. This, as well as his invincible stupidity, is Bottom's protection in the wild world of the wood. Just like the lovers, the mechanicals do not enter the wood naked and afraid; they take a language with them.

Naming names will be an important matter for the mechanicals all through, and certainly in the interlude itself. Names are their safety, the insurance policy of literalism which will save them from giving offence and in the process cause such hilarious damage to dramatic illusion. Quince, as the patient, beleaguered director of this company, is the type of every producer of every amateur company – diplomatic, anxious and occasionally testy, but inclined to appeasement in the case of his star player. With such economy of arrangements did Shakespeare make a setting for Bully Bottom.

Nick Bottom is one of the greatest comic roles in Shakespeare and offers massive opportunities to the actor. In all the scope for diversity of playing, however, we can say that certain characteristics are so firmly written into the part that no good performance could omit them. For the actors who play the mechanicals, the Act V interlude will offer the enticing challenge of successfully portraying bad acting, not the easiest of performance tasks. For the actor playing Bottom this is the task throughout, with the additional test and delight that Bottom does not actually make a total mess of all his assigned roles. There is a little area of unexpected triumph about Nick Bottom. He owes it to the fact that he is indeed a compulsive actor. He simply cannot resist the attractions of a part. By natural instinct and character, he is a man of the theatre. Also, he cannot act. This seemingly unfortunate combination is the hilarious saving of Bottom the Weaver.

Bottom's propensity for acting is apparent in Act I scene ii when the woodland rehearsal is first mooted. Like the most egocentric of amateur actors, he wants to play all the parts, even those that do not exist. His unsolicited audition piece as Ercles the tyrant (Bottom's name for Theseus' kinsman, Hercules) gives Shakespeare the pretext for professional satire at the expense of the bombastic post-Senecan tragedy so recently in fashion, and the comic echo of a superseded theatrical idiom should, in Bottom's voice, be as loud and extravagant as the actor can make it. After this distracting performance his instant return from Ercles to Nick Bottom is wholly in character; first the self-congratulation of 'This was lofty!' and then the practicality, 'Now name the rest of the players', as if others and not he were to blame for holding things up. Before the scene is over he has experimented with Thisbe and probably also with two sorts of leonine roaring, the ferocious kind and the birdlike kind. Bottom's complacency, his complete conviction of his power to move audiences, his actual power to move them unintentionally, his would-be professionalism, his obsessive theatricality, and his serious humour – all are established in the mechanicals' first scene. In particular we notice that his love of extravagant roles has spilt over into his own speaking voice, notably in his penchant for needless repetitions and for putting his own superior words in the place of other people's.

These various instructions to the real-life actor are confirmed in Act III scene i, when they arrive in the wood, augmented by the primary habit of unbreakable literalism which is to be the central feature of all subsequent appearances. Yet there is a possible counter-effect here, which is certainly reinforced later. Quince and company are much concerned with the theatrical necessity of moonlight. It is dim Snug who suggests that the problem might be solved by *literal* moonlight, and sets them leafing through the almanac. When they find that the moon does indeed shine on the night of their play, it is Bottom who says:

Why, then, may you leave a casement of the Great Chamber window – where we play – open, and the moon may shine in at the casement.

(III.i.50–52)

If we postulate a true Great Chamber in which *A Midsummer Night's Dream* was first performed to a courtly audience, and the not entirely fanciful contingency of open casements and moonlight, Bottom's literalism is a window to the magical. An audience watching theatricals about players rehearsing theatricals, for an audience whose audience they were, would find all the layers of theatrical distancing momentarily

97

abolished by the actuality of moonlight – an instant of confused enchantment which brings together theatre, imagination and the real. It is only a hypothetical possibility, but it exists. If so, it is Bottom's doing. His mundane theatrical invention has accidentally crossed the border to imagination, and not for the last time in the play. Such an effect, if indeed it happened, would be isolated and confirmed by the immediate reductive comedy of 'the person of Moonshine' – Quince's invention, which is by contrast totally devoid of imagination, accidental or real.

The play with literalism takes on its deeper comic form with Puck's joke, and Bottom's transformation to an ass. Bottom is asinine indeed, but he can cope. The comedy of literal and metaphoric asses is introduced here and is intermittently repeated for the rest of the play. Bottom's appearance with his ass's head, and poor Snout's amazement, provoke the weaver's remonstrance, 'You see an ass head of your own, do you?' Their flight 'is to make an ass of me'. Later, his skin tickled by the hair, he is 'such a tender ass'. At last, awakening, he declares 'Man is but an ass if he go about to expound this dream.' To see the point of this verbal comedy we do not require Jan Kott's assurance that the ass is a sexual wonder, or anachronistic phonological plays on 'ass' and 'arse'. What matters is that Bottom is using *metaphors* each time about something which, unknown to him, is literally true. With comic colloquial banality Bottom is unconsciously breaking free of the literal, without realizing how deeply he is stuck in it. The mechanicals' comedy of idiotic literalism, which is centred on Bottom, is all the funnier because it inadvertently transcends itself; so when Demetrius, among the clever audience of Act V, tells Theseus that one lion may speak 'when many asses do', the joke is on him.

Bottom's personal role, in fact, is a singular and real example of the interlude's eventual effect. It is an idiotic extravaganza, compulsively theatrical in nature, where invention operates without imagination and is incorrigibly literalist in substance, yet is imaginative by chance.

When we look at Bottom's encounter with the fairies, in two scenes wonderfully made of farce and poignancy, we find a Bottom who does not do at all badly. His very shortcomings – his complacency and self-centredness and (not incompatibly) common sense, his lack of imagination and defective acting – make him *more* rather than less adaptable to his new surroundings. Bottom copes with the wood much better than the lovers do, and the comparison is an apt one because there are careful situational and thematic resemblances between the parallel sets of woodland experiences. These can be effectively considered in terms of style and language.

There are several circumstances in the play where language is especially dynamic. There are points where one language modulates into another, changing key and tempo, within a character-group (as it does in Act I scene i when the lovers are left on their own). There are points where two languages meet and coexist (as they do pre-eminently in Act V, but also at earlier moments, especially those contrived or influenced by Puck). And there are times when characters are placed at border points, stranded between 'dreaming' and waking, as the lovers are when Theseus has aroused them in Act IV. These last are important moments, when the characters' states of mind are like Miranda's memory of her girlhood:

> 'Tis far off,
> And rather like a dream than an assurance
> That my remembrance warrants.
> *(The Tempest*, I.ii.44–6)

Bottom's language has equivalents of all these dynamisms, and at times has comparable thematic importance. In the scenes he shares with the other mechanicals, his sudden mock-transcendences, his take-offs into theatrical rhetoric, contrast with the earthbound prose of the others. Peter Quince does not waste words at all except when appeasing Bottom, whereupon wasted words are his only hope. Bottom himself moves fluently between the registers, at home in his own 'mind' and wholly innocent of the comic incongruities he perpetrates. With his fellows he speaks a mobile language in a static group. The coexistent languages, when members of character-groups meet each other, have their richest comic expression in the relationship between Bottom and Titania. And Bottom's own 'border point', his awakening from the dream, follows that of the lovers at the end of Act IV scene i, in one of the greatest speeches of the play.

Bottom's coexistent language with Titania displays admirably the virtues of his limitations. Titania, wakening under the influence of the love juice, declares her love for Bottom and attributes it to the effect of his visual beauty. His response is sententious, self-admiring, unimaginative, generalized and foolishly sagacious. Also true. As for loving him:

Methinks, mistress, you should have little reason for that. And yet, to say the truth, reason and love keep little company together nowadays – the more the pity that some honest neighbours will not make them friends. – Nay, I can gleek upon occasion.

(III.i.135–9)

This is the response of the simple-shrewd Athenian artisan. Thematically, however, it naturally connects us with the world of the lovers and their efforts to account for love's abrupt irrationalities in terms of reason; and with Theseus, whose containment within reason's values causes him to relegate, if not deny, whole areas of confused experience. In a play of such voices Bottom's moralism is good sense: he points to a division which exists, and perceives a difficult and yet desirable reconciliation of love with reason, the achievement of which is at the heart of the play. Moreover, he is modest, and his shortage of imagination serves him well. He will not take Titania's delusion seriously, despite the flattery it offers to his capacious ego. Threatened with compliments to his wisdom and beauty, his reaction is the same as Helena's (see III.ii.314–16) – disbelief, and anxiety to get out of the wood with a safe skin. His speech has its important place in the play's dialogue of love and reason.

In these scenes of co-existent languages, Bottom's literalism serves him well in circumstances which again set up a parallel with the lovers, and show him in a far from unimpressive light. His dealings with the minor fairies are Bottom's triumph. Adaptable as his stupidity allows him to be, he takes quite readily to the acquisition of fairy attendants. Sublimely unsurprised, he takes them at their word, and their word is chiefly a name. Nay, they must name their names, just as the names of the mechanicals and their parts were lovingly spoken earlier. 'Cobweb', 'Peaseblossom' and 'Mustardseed' are important as names; he asks each of them in turn. Each reply he takes quite literally. Cobwebs are used to stop bleeding, so Bottom will know where to go with a cut finger; Peaseblossom is agriculturally connected; Mustardseed is tasty with beef. Nothing will prise Bottom out of the literal. However, he treats his unexpected fairy servants with immaculate courtesy, repetitively asking their names and desiring more acquaintance. He is polite, condescendingly respectful and scrupulously equal in his dealings. While the lovers, nobly trained in the disciplines of Athenian courtesy, are setting poor examples in the parallel scenes, Bottom's faultless good manners to the fairies are a comic positive, very funny, very incongruous, and very right. He is seen at his best in Act IV scene i, wholly unbothered by the miniaturization of the fairies except to be concerned for their welfare; he would be 'loath to have [Cobweb] overflown with a honey bag, signor'. Improbable ideals of right order are hidden in the comic grotesqueries of Bottom's woodland eminence.

Bottom's greatest moment comes at his 'border point', when at the end of Act IV scene i he awakens from his 'dream'. This is his dii equivalent of the lovers' wakening, which has just preceded it. He and the four lovers have all slept during their 'dream', though only Hermia has actually dreamed. Like Lysander and Demetrius, Bottom has undergone a transformation under Puck's ministrations and has been restored before daylight to a former state. Like the lovers, he remembers his experience only as a dream. The lovers woke with divided selves and a sense of receding wonders. For Bottom, however, the sense of wonder is transcendent. Commentators now recognize the mangled version in his speech of Paul's First Epistle to the Corinthians (2: 9):

But as it is written, Eye hath not seen, nor ear heard, neither have entered into the heart of man, the things which God hath prepared for them that love him.

Any risk of blasphemy is removed by the comic dislocations of sense and of senses in Bottom's version:

The eye of man hath not heard, the ear of man hath not seen, man's hand is not able to taste, his tongue to conceive, nor his heart to report what my dream was!

(IV.i.208–11)

Dislocations of the senses occur several times in *A Midsummer Night's Dream*, their chief effect being to dislodge the eye from its primacy (see Chapter 5), but this is the most extended instance. In the darkness of the wood the eye is no longer dominant, and as other senses come into prominence their data is mistakenly referred to it by the sensuously habit-formed body, an effect captured to perfection by Keats in the 'Ode to a Nightingale':

> I cannot see what flowers are at my feet
> Nor what soft incense hangs upon the boughs.

With the eye's authority overridden, other modes of perception come into play, both through the other senses as mediators and organs of transmission (hence the truth underlying the comic play with reallocated sensory roles) and through the superior powers of internal 'vision' for which the eye is only a neutral agent. In so far as *A Midsummer Night's Dream* is about competing ways of knowing and competing modes of judgement, Bottom's speech is important to it, and its source in Corinthians gives particular importance to the heart. The passage from Paul is about divine mysteries, the existence of wonders beyond the power of humankind to perceive or know. Bottom's comic-serious visionary wakening subtly adapts this verse. These sensory events have indeed not occurred as Bottom relates them, because he is a confused man describing confusion. But he is also, for a moment, a deeply moved man who is trying, and inevitably failing, to find words for something that has truly entered his heart. The heart cannot, in Bottom's speech, *report* what it has received; but the experience, even if it cannot be held once day and reason and normality have returned, has nevertheless occurred. These borderland speeches of awakening are the nearest that Shakespeare gets, in this case daringly so, to claiming a religious validation for his drama's visionary centre. In this scene, more unmistakably than anywhere else perhaps, this early comedy looks forward to the late romances.

The dream 'shall be called "Bottom's Dream", because it hath no bottom'. The self-admiring pun preserves the comedy, and the ambiguity is neat: either there is nothing to it, or else it is unfathomably deep. Bottom's impulse as he wakes up is to preserve his dream by turning it into a ballad; that is to say by turning it into art, and performing it in a play. Nick Bottom the compulsive actor is true to himself. His very first thought on waking up was for the play ('When my cue comes, call me, and I will answer'), but this too is capable of more presumptuous interpretation, if we choose to observe a secular transcendence or displaced religious vision in the speech. For a moment, perhaps, Bottom – like the lovers moments earlier, but more so – is 'beside himself'. As he goes off, it is in the theatre that he thinks of reporting these things. Neither he nor the lovers are capable, as it turns out, of retaining them except as dreams and remembered illusions; but by these means the theatricality of Act V is linked to the vision of the middle scenes, their agent of connection being the simple, literalist and splendidly adaptable actor in the wood.

The fairies

One of the best discussions of the fairies is Ernest Schanzer's, passages from whose article 'The Moon and the Fairies in *A Midsummer Night's Dream*' are reprinted in the Macmillan *Casebook* collection. 'In this play,' Schanzer writes, 'we are given three wholly distinct kinds of fairies, provided we can speak of Puck as a fairy at all', and he notes that Puck 'considers himself to be a fairy'. However, Puck is an anomalous figure in the play, partly of the fairy world and partly not, and his language as well as his intermediate mode of being put him in a special place, deserving separate consideration.

There are certainly, including Puck, three distinct kinds of inhabitants of the fairy world, and Puck is probably the least original. Shakespeare's Puck is a fine elaboration of Robin Goodfellow's traditional role in folklore, while the others are something quite new. 'In the case of the fairies,' wrote G. K. Hunter, 'Shakespeare is to be credited with the creation, single-handed, of an entirely new world', and it is 'both benevolent and mysterious'. The miniaturization of the attendant fairies is Shakespeare's deliberate choice (though not his invention), and so is the blend of mystery and benevolence in Oberon and Titania. Elsewhere in folk tradition there were other kinds of fairies, malign and destructive beings, from whom Oberon and Titania are at pains to distance themselves.

Schanzer, as I quoted him earlier, says of the miniature fairies that nothing 'could be more misleading than to speak of them as irresponsible children, as so many critics do ...' Irresponsible they are not, but children they surely are. Whether or not they were originally played by children of a noble house at a marriage feast, they were certainly played by boys at subsequent public performances by Shakespeare's company. They are very responsible and orderly children, extremely well brought up. In a play which depends so heavily on symmetry of character-groups, and interchangeability of character within almost identical adult companies, nowhere is the symmetry and identity more complete than with the miniature fairies, 'adult' servants in childlike form. Bottom's courteous and careful treatment of them is that of someone who knows how to treat children. The dialogue of Cobweb, Peaseblossom and Mustardseed is absolutely identical. 'Ready', 'Hail', and the naming of their names is the sum of it. They respond to Bottom's summons with a darting eagerness of voice which is libretto and choreography alike. The voice must be quick, light and choric, and accompanied by a rhythmic alacrity of responsive movement. Only children could give the effect of innocent clustering which the text prescribes for them. That is not to say that other ways of playing the minor fairies are impossible – just eccentric. The use of adult male actors as the fairies in some recent productions is one of the least convincing repudiations of romantic performance traditions.

Aside from their response to Bottom, the presence of the minor fairies is chiefly physical and musical; they dance with Oberon and Titania at the dawn reunion and the wedding blessing, they sing at the blessing, and they sing the lullaby to Titania in Act II scene ii. Their role is to be harmonious, obedient and protective; they are the literal embodiment of voluntary concord.

All this is thematically important, especially the lullaby. This is just as much an exorcism as the fairy blessing for the human lovers at the end of the play, and it also shows the hierarchic ordering of fairy powers. The fairies plead 'Nor spell nor charm/Come our lovely lady nigh', but the exorcism is powerless against the intrusive spells of Oberon, who is there as soon as the coast is clear with his love juice. Moreover, Oberon in his campaign of retributive blackmail summons wild beasts to be the objects of Titania's dotage. It may seem that the fairies' song is melodiously futile.

There are counter-currents, though. The creatures against which the fairies invoke protection are of the kind which in *Macbeth* makes up the witches' brew: snake, newt and blindworm. It is not ferocious wildness but insidious creaturely venom which the fairies name as a threat. Not all the natural world is similarly hostile: Philomel, the nightingale, is enlisted to join the song, and birds, like minor fairies, are beneficent and harmless. (Bottom will 'roar you an 'twere any nightingale'.) More importantly, the fact of music is itself a promise of calm order, despite its seeming inefficacy. Oberon's ritualistic temporary malice is pre-attuned by healing melody.

All the same, the Fairy Queen is not invulnerable. Oberon's vengeful magic may be 'placed' by the lullaby, but the fairies' purpose was indeed protective and not merely sleep-inducing. The fairies are not in full command of their wild world, not even in the persons of the Fairy King and Queen. They generate disorders from within themselves and cause lateral discordances which reflect their own unseemly quarrelling. When Titania, in her great aria on the unseasonable seasons, speaks of the revengeful winds made angry by neglect and disregard, she is declaring the place and limitations of fairy powers. The natural spirits commanded by Oberon and Titania are creatures of loyalty, but not of slavery and bondage, and they are capable of misrule. When the natural order is properly harmonious, its right expression is in music and in dance; but when there is a breach in the monarchic balance, these forces have minds of their own to take offence. Oberon and Titania can decree a natural harmony only by their mutual condition as it truly is, and not by unilateral benevolent ordering. Hence, in the world of danger generated by her dispute with Oberon, Titania is at risk from the venomous creatures of a very different spiritual order, from which she and Oberon disassociate themselves. The scene of the lullaby and the spell is thematically linked to the nature of fairy power in the play, and in particular to the power of Oberon. In the full spectrum of the play's ideas it restricts still further the limited reach of human reason and human understanding. There is a mystery beyond the mysteries, a phenomenon of power which is not fully circumscribed even by Oberon and Titania, but lies beyond the full control of fairy rule. Paradoxically, Oberon and Titania are the *embodiment* of powers which are greater than the power they themselves exercise (rather like modern constitutional monarchs!).

The language of Titania and Oberon is extremely impressive. Most of the arias considered earlier are theirs. Repeatedly it is Oberon and Titania who send the play into spirals of enfranchising imagination, taking it beyond the confines of Athens and the palace wood, away on global and even inter-stellar passages of mind. They are the evokers of the Indian beach and the promontory, in sustained passages of expansive vision. Their speech can be solemn, leisurely and meditative, but their intelligence remains in full play even within a vocabulary of sensuous recall. Spaciousness of imaginative geography and verbal spaciousness are inseparable, and these apparently decorative, superfluous speeches cannot be cut without a forfeiture of perspective which does great damage to the play's meaning. Yet their language is also full of speed, taking us on exhilarating flights of global instancy. Even when Titania's retinue are dismissed on errands, they are permitted absence only for 'the third part of a minute'. In the distinctive speech that Shakespeare gives the King and Queen, imperiousness is lyrical in nature. The movement they incite (because both Oberon and Titania are Shakespeare's surrogate choreographers for the fairies and for Puck) is light, athletic, swift and buoyant. It is also fused with images of scale. The fairies traverse delicate terrains of air, between vast exotic orient landscapes and the minutely observed interiors of English flowers.

Oberon and Titania are natural intelligences, and in Oberon's language especially we encounter meticulous observation translated into power. The nature of that power, in the thematic design of the play, can only be clarified by matching him with Theseus; they are contrasting, complementary, necessary figures. But the power of each is limited, and the play suggests, at times disturbingly, the existence of forces which neither can contain.

Puck

Puck is less obviously a part for a child to play than the fairies are, but there is a long if intermittent record of the role being played by children. Ellen Terry played Puck as a child in the mid-nineteenth century (and broke her toe in the process, when a trapdoor was prematurely closed on her foot as she made a spectacular entrance for the final scene). Certain

105

of the fairies' characteristics are writ large in Puck. Their speed and agility, the physical élan of swift obedience, the pleasure of athletic instancy that cancels out all traces of mere servitude – these are Puck's qualities as much as those of the fairies, and he has more opportunities to show them. There are dramatic advantages in a diminutive gymnastic Puck, provided that attractive impishness is a part but not the whole of the resulting performance. There is a great deal more to Puck than mischief.

He calls himself a fairy, and is indeed as much the supernatural creature and prompt attendant upon Oberon as the minor fairies are for Titania. Whilst they are unrebellious spirits, however, Puck is a law unto himself. As befits his different ancestry, descending as he does from the independent mischievous spirit Robin Goodfellow of English folklore, he enjoys a different relationship with the human as well as the supernatural figures of the play. Reginald Scot's *The Discoverie of Witchcraft* (1584) names him as the hobgoblin of popular superstition and anticipates the ambiguous nature of his disposition as Shakespeare draws it. Primarily a prankster, taking delight in humiliating tricks on helpless humans, he is also capable of good deeds and a kind of furtive benevolence. Like the whole fairy kingdom he is able to cause harm as well as good to humankind, but he has his idiosyncratic way of doing it. In the end benevolence is uppermost, but it is the contemptuous benevolence of a tricksy spirit who is chiefly self-delighting. He does not cause the night's unruliness, at any rate where the lovers are concerned, but he enjoys it.

Puck's role, in fact, is extraordinarily comprehensive. He is Oberon's servant and always physically obedient (hence the adult actor's task of conveying a childlike springiness of free servitude), but he is fully capable of answering back when reproved, refusing to accept sole responsibility for a mistake which is largely Oberon's and openly expressing a divergent glee when things go wrong. The relationship between them, as revealed by the discovery of the love juice error, is important for Puck's wider position in the play:

> OBERON   Of thy misprision must perforce ensue
> Some true love turned, and not a false turned true.
> PUCK   Then fate o'errules, that, one man holding truth,
> A million fail, confounding oath on oath.
>
>   (III.ii.90–93)

Puck turns Oberon's accusation into a self-defensive generalization, but not in the tone of one who stands in need of excuses. Rather, he echoes Oberon's style and verse-form with a mocking purpose, seizing the opportunity to make cynical observations about the love foibles of humankind. He knows the human race more intimately than Oberon does.

Puck, in fact, is the play's great intermediary. He is the go-between, connecting the fairy world with the human, appropriately (in view of his nature) charged with converting the theoretical goodwill of fairy powers into erratic practice. His task is to be the minister for higher powers, to be the immaculate observer's dutiful executant, the profane and comic instrument of an unlikely providence. Since the chosen means of service is the contrivance of love affairs, he performs this in ways which do eventually turn out well. In the acting of it, however, he loses no opportunity for incidental ridicule. Disorientated physical confusion is Puck's favourite device: first setting the frightened mechanicals in clumsy flight through the wood, and later enjoying the delights of human mimicry to lead Demetrius and Lysander on exhausting wild goose chases in the darkness. Much of the audience's pleasure in the spectacle of their own kind's absurdity is contrived for them by Puck. The character of irrational lunacy in love is of the human race's own making, but its conversion into situational comedy is a matter for Puck. He it is who turns the theory of irrationality into theatre.

This is the second dimension of Puck's performance as an intermediary. Not only does he arrange the misconnections and the eventual kindly joinings between fairy world and human, but he does the same between play and audience. When he meets the mechanicals, embarked on their rehearsal in the wood, his reaction is one of opportunist connoisseurship at this choice spectacle of human daftness and the chance to use it:

> What hempen homespuns have we swaggering here
> So near the cradle of the Fairy Queen?
> What, a play toward? I'll be an auditor –
> An actor too, perhaps, if I see cause.

(III.i.70–73)

Puck is a social conservative despite his anarchic pleasures. His opinion of humanity at large is fairly low, but he still has a sense of appropriate distinctions. This lot are yokels, very different from Theseus. As special fools within a foolish race, they are a delicacy for mockers. Puck knows the right order of the fairy world, too. He may be Oberon's intelligencer, and Oberon may be estranged from Titania, but Puck is still mildly outraged by this gross trespassing upon Titania's bower. There is order within anarchy in Puck, so the audience is not troubled by too malignant an iconoclast. Therefore his further role as audience can quite readily enlist the real-life audience's connivance. For audience he does indeed propose to be – and actor. Puck's spying on this thespian folly clarifies the audience's own. He is the play's first audience-on-stage. Intervening, as he then does, as an 'actor' in this interlude, he teaches us about the interventionist spectator.

This comically splendid incident therefore has its resonances for the play as a whole. It is an indispensable link in that subtle connection between two roles that we see enacted on the stage: that of the observer (pre-eminently Oberon) and that of the audience-on-stage (the married couples of Act V). Both roles involve interventionist, participant watchers; both, as we have argued elsewhere, are watching different forms of the play-within-a-play. Puck, in this fine episode, is doing all these things; he is relishing as active observer the enactment by the mechanicals of what becomes (because of his presence) both an intended and an unintended play. In the layering of audience response which is at the heart of *A Midsummer Night's Dream*'s dramatic method, this scene is indispensable. To confirm its multiple nature, Puck's lines are spoken in formal blank verse. His status is momentarily high, and his interposed theatrical critique ('A stranger Pyramus than e'er played here') anticipates the courtly heckling of the Act V audience.

Puck's diverse role as intermediary, then, has a major impact on the total effect of the play. As Lysander and Helena approach (III.ii.110–22) in the toils of the farcical courtship that the fairies' error has caused, Puck invites his master to join him in the pleasures of audience, and gives the independent verdict that his special closeness to humanity has warranted:

> Shall we their fond pageant see?
> Lord, what fools these mortals be!
> (III.ii.114–15)

An effective performance of *A Midsummer Night's Dream* must surely win approval for this statement, not primarily from Oberon (who is distinctly cooler in his acquiescence) but from us. The audience should find itself accepting Puck's outspoken verdict on humanity because it enjoys temporary diplomatic immunity by virtue of its status as an audience. For us as spectators *A Midsummer Night's Dream* is a comic masterpiece of protected self-confrontation, and Puck is the supreme agent of this effect. Seen here at its most direct, it is a quality of audience response which permeates the play, especially Act V.

I have referred briefly elsewhere to the range of verse-forms that Puck is given. They include, as in these quotations, the play's dominant forms – the blank verse iambic pentameter and the trochaic tetrameter in rhyming couplets – but he also has rhyming pentameters, and a remarkable collection of forms in his last speech in Act III scene ii, as he squeezes the love juice on Lysander's eyes and finally sets things right. These are *not* just virtuoso displays on Shakespeare's part; they reflect the very wide range of tones, moods and occasions that the role of Puck must verbally (and physically) encompass. This last speech, for example, must stretch from the incantatory spellmaking of 'On the ground/Sleep sound' to the rollicking easy animalism of 'The man shall have his mare again, and all shall be well'. Puck's greatest speech, his last before the epilogue, employs another technical variation, the trochaic tetrameter in quatrains. With 'Now the hungry lion roars' Puck is finally both the familiar domestic spirit and the unfathomable mystery, and the world he evokes is the most concentrated expression of this comedy's unique fusion of blessing and danger.

5. Imagery

Throughout this study attention has repeatedly fallen on the physical theatricality of *A Midsummer Night's Dream*. Within the drama plays are performed, knowingly and unknowingly, and actor-spectators watch moving figures; the pattern of the action is dancelike, and the human movement that we see has the energy and animation of dance itself; there are characters in physical or vocal conflict with each other, and they are individual representatives of larger or more patterned confrontations; the speech itself is so varied, so idiosyncratic and yet in all its diversity so regular that it takes on the quality of music. In all these ways it is easy to see the play's dynamic quality as theatre. If we turn to imagery and look at the verbal recurrences – the ideas-made-objects which are symbols in dramatic poetry – it is harder to argue that these will have similar impact and immediacy for an audience. If we are not careful, the dramatic poem can seem to subdue the play, and effects emerge which may be demonstrable in the study or the classroom, but are much less obvious to an audience busy with events and action. All the same, the existence of coherent patterns, repetitions and clusters of images in Shakespearean drama is long established and generally accepted, and all commentators on Shakespeare owe an enormous debt in particular to Caroline Spurgeon, Wolfgang Clemen and Wilson Knight for their pioneering work in this field of Shakespeare studies.

Before we turn to the particular dominant images of *A Midsummer Night's Dream*, it is perhaps worth emphasizing that imagery is not a separate poetic 'item' in a Shakespeare text, detached from its theatrical life and present only as a poetic embellishment, or a symbolic vocabulary for ideas and themes. Most of Shakespeare's important groups and clusters of images have their physical analogues in the action. For example, the tempest imagery of the plays is matched by the central event of an actual storm, and the behaviour of people on that play is accompanied by the spectacle of people on stage suffering like creatures in pain or fear that play is especially of clothing which is in two senses of the word like condition of animals. The repeated imagery of clothing in *Macbeth* accompanied by the physical spectacle of Macbeth wearing a crown robes to which we know he is not entitled, and continuing to wear as their symbolic eminence becomes less and less commensurate with his

110

5. Imagery

Throughout this study attention has repeatedly fallen on the physical theatricality of *A Midsummer Night's Dream*. Within the drama plays are performed, knowingly and unknowingly, and actor-spectators watch moving figures; the pattern of the action is dancelike, and the human movement that we see has the energy and animation of dance itself; there are characters in physical or vocal conflict with each other, and they are individual representatives of larger or more patterned confrontations; the speech itself is so varied, so idiosyncratic and yet in all its diversity so regular that it takes on the quality of music. In all these ways it is easy to see the play's dynamic quality as theatre. If we turn to imagery and look at the verbal recurrences – the ideas-made-objects which are symbols in dramatic poetry – it is harder to argue that these will have similar impact and immediacy for an audience. If we are not careful, the dramatic poem can seem to subdue the play, and effects emerge which may be demonstrable in the study or the classroom, but are much less obvious to an audience busy with events and action. All the same, the existence of coherent patterns, repetitions and clusters of images in Shakespearean drama is long established and generally accepted, and all commentators on Shakespeare owe an enormous debt in particular to Caroline Spurgeon, Wolfgang Clemen and Wilson Knight for their pioneering work in this field of Shakespeare studies.

Before we turn to the particular dominant images of *A Midsummer Night's Dream*, it is perhaps worth emphasizing that imagery is not a separate poetic 'item' in a Shakespeare text, detached from its theatrical life and present only as a poetic embellishment, or a symbolic vocabulary for ideas and themes. Most of Shakespeare's important groups and clusters of images have their physical parallels and analogues in the action. For example, the tempest imagery of *King Lear* is matched by the central event of an actual storm, and the beast imagery of that play is accompanied by the spectacle of people on the stage behaving like predatory beasts, suffering like creatures in pain or reduced to the naked condition of animals. The repeated imagery of clothing in *Macbeth*, and especially of clothing which is in two senses of the word 'unfitting', is accompanied by the physical spectacle of Macbeth wearing a crown and robes to which we know he is not entitled, and continuing to wear them as their symbolic eminence becomes less and less commensurate with his is given. They include, as in these quotations, the play's dominant forms – the blank verse iambic pentameter and the trochaic tetrameter in rhyming couplets – but he also has rhyming pentameters, and a remarkable collection of forms in his last speech in Act III scene ii, as he squeezes the love juice on Lysander's eyes and finally sets things right. These are *not* just virtuoso displays on Shakespeare's part; they reflect the very wide range of tones, moods and occasions that the role of Puck must verbally (and physically) encompass. This last speech, for example, must stretch from the incantatory spellmaking of 'On the ground/Sleep sound' to the rollicking easy animalism of 'The man shall have his mare again, and all shall be well'. Puck's greatest speech, his last before the epilogue, employs another technical variation, the trochaic tetrameter in quatrains. With 'Now the hungry lion roars' Puck is finally both the familiar domestic spirit and the unfathomable mystery, and the world he evokes is the most concentrated expression of this comedy's unique fusion of blessing and danger.

desperate, embattled and ignoble condition. The inner state of the man, although exciting tragic pity, is profoundly at odds with the symbolic meaning of his garments and regalia.

In *A Midsummer Night's Dream*, perhaps the most theatrically physical of all Shakespeare's plays, it is not surprising to find a similar correspondence between the dominant images and the visual and active elements of the play. This is one of the earliest of Shakespeare's plays in which he uses rich groupings or clusters of images as a means of reinforcing dramatic statement; this will become a customary dramatic method and a major aid to interpretation in his later work. All are directly linked to the drama's physical embodiment, those parts of its theatricality which no audience can miss.

By general consent the most important images in the play are the moon and moonlight. The play begins and ends in Athens, but the central action takes place in the wood, by night. Whatever the performance circumstances of the play, its imaginative placement is in glimmering night, when all light comes from natural sources, the moon and the stars. We may speculate about the first performance, which could have been at night, with actual moonlight as a magical nearby reality for the Great Chamber audience, but most of the performances in public, which clearly proved so popular, took place in the open, in the afternoon, in broad daylight. The moonlight depends upon the dramatist's skill and the audience's imagination. So powerful is this factor that the nature of theatrical illusion and audience imagination becomes a major theme of the play, directly before us whenever the mechanicals are around but reaching full thematic dominance in Act V. The audience, in collusion with the dramatist, creates the moonlight. Plot and situation in themselves require it, and the essential dramatic illusion is powerfully supported by physical activity and burlesque.

The ways in which the lovers and the mechanicals move are part of this simple but necessary process. In the opening Athenian scenes their movements (though sharply differentiated in style and grace) are physically confident and assured – they know exactly where they are. As soon as they reach the grove by night, these physical certainties are taken away. Instead we have an inimitable mixture of felt disorder and dancelike patterning, of confusion as the characters experience it within a comic, aesthetic order which they neither know nor understand. This conjunction of order and disorder gives the middle scenes their special quality. One way and another there is a great deal of anxious scampering about in half-light, more strongly physically present to us because it contrasts with the swift and confident physical grace of Puck and the

111

fairies. This is precisely the condition of human beings in moonlight, and the moon itself is the light which implies a darkness. The light is magical, beautiful, silver and unearthly, sometimes enough to see by and sometimes not. For human beings it is not their natural environment of light but a disorientating luminousness, one which threatens dangers but also offers the prospect of visions and transformations.

The imagined physical context of moonlight is made the more seductive in its magic by the mechanicals' problems with the task of *staging* moonlight. Real moonlight through the casement is one answer, but real moonlight is only magical if it is also imaginative moonlight. The nature of theatre is such that literalism alone is merely absurd; the imagination must accede to it before it can become truth. The imaginative collusion which drama requires is made comically plain by the catastrophic alternative device which poor Starveling is lumbered with. No one will believe this futile illusory contrivance. On the other hand, the moon as a poetic and imaginative potency is there in its truth from the opening lines of the play, as Theseus and Hippolyta argue about its cyclical regularity. Lunar movement is the play's first fact, and it is not subservient to human impatience, even the impatience of betrothed dukes.

Out of this context of imaginative physicality, laid before us in clear stage circumstances, the moon takes on its multiple significances as an image, and as audience we respond to these unconsciously and intuitively because they are integral with the drama's physical setting. From the very beginning the moon is a measure of time. She suggests regularity of change, movement within predictability, the harmonious order of time's passage. This in turn gives astronomic sanction to the process of decay and renewal, end and beginning, which is part of the human condition. Fairies can excel her speed – the fairy who first meets Puck can wander 'swifter than the moon's sphere', and the reconciled Oberon and Titania can fly 'swifter than the wandering moon' – but neither fairies nor humans can alter the regularity of lunar waxing and waning.

As well as symbolizing regularity of change, the moon (with no logical inconsistency of suggestion) also stands for constancy; 'she serves,' noted Caroline Spurgeon, 'for an emblem of steadfast constancy; and Hermia cries she would as soon believe a hole might be bored in the centre of the earth and the moon creep through it, as that Lysander should willingly have left her' (*Shakespeare's Imagery* (1935), p. 260). Sometimes the natural and the mythic functions of the moon are difficult to separate, notably in Titania's great 'seasons' speech where, in the course of describing the seasonal disorders produced by her quarrel with Oberon, she says:

> Therefore the moon, the governess of floods,
> Pale in her anger, washes all the air,
> That rheumatic diseases do abound . . .
>
> (II.i.103–5)

The moon is here personified, but not necessarily deified. Titania's speech is filled with vivid personifications suggesting orderly natural forms provoked into ill-tempered vengefulness by their resentment of the quarrel. In the context of the speech the moon is only one (albeit an important one) of these. The moon is the natural force which controls the tides, and as such is chief amongst the many dissentient parts of nature which have devastated human life with untimely excess of water.

On the other hand, the moon is also a goddess with deep roots in mythology, and it may be implicitly in this deistic form that the moon, as Luna or Phoebe, has exerted the offended powers of a superior deity over Oberon and Titania, with humanity as innocent, uncomprehending victim. Either way the powers of Oberon and Titania, considerable as they are, are limited. The moon, whether as goddess or natural force, is not within their control.

In the mythological background of the play, the moon is one form of the triple goddess Luna, Diana and Hecate – Luna is her form as moon goddess, Diana her form as earth goddess, and Hecate her form as goddess of the underworld. Both Luna (or Phoebe) the moon goddess, and Diana the earth goddess, are goddesses of chastity, and in this way also the image of the moon is essential to the play's pattern of ideas. When Hermia is threatened by Theseus with a sentence of perpetual chastity, she is to live 'Chanting faint hymns to the cold fruitless moon', and the place of her vow will be 'Diana's altar', sacred to the earthly form of the triple goddess. The moon's identification with chastity is subtly deterrent here, but in Oberon's famous 'imperial votaress' speech (II.i.155–74) it is celebratory, as befits a tribute to the Queen. Luna and Diana, here as elsewhere, are bent on frustrating the pranks of the mischievous love god Cupid, and Oberon saw Cupid's arrow 'Quenched in the chaste beams of the watery moon'. Later, as Titania leads Bottom away on the unchaste project of her infatuated desire, she sees the moon look 'with a watery eye . . . Lamenting some enforcèd chastity'.

Conversely, however, Luna and Diana are also patronesses of fertility and childbirth, and the double nature of the goddess is part of the mythological background for the double concept of chastity – chastity as virginal abstention and chastity as procreative fulfilment within faithful marriage – which has been discussed. Harold F. Brooks, in his introduction to the New Arden Shakespeare edition, therefore comments rightly that the 'regency of the moon bridges the contrast between the ideal virginity of the imperial votaress, and the ideal of fertile marriage celebrated in the conclusion toward which the play has moved from the beginning' (p. cxxx).

The moon is also associated with madness, and infiltrates the play's concern with the madness and irrationality of love, not least through Theseus' famous grouping together of 'The lunatic, the lover and the poet'.

In Titania's 'seasons' speech the moon as 'governess of floods' was linked to an unhealthy and ruinous saturation of the land and air, but the association of the moon with water is a frequent, usually innocent and joyous one throughout the play. In both the references to the moon as a symbol of chastity, quoted above, she was described as 'watery'. The connection of images is carried further in Lysander's lines:

> Tomorrow night, when Phoebe doth behold
> Her silver image in the watery glass,
> Decking with liquid pearl the bladed grass . . .
>
> (I.i.209–11)

The moon, in the play, is the cause of dew, and dewdrops in their turn are the natural equivalent in beauty and preciousness of jewels. Dew is almost sacred: Oberon's final speech of blessing in the play instructs the fairies to bless the marriage chambers with 'this field dew consecrate'. Certainly it has the value of jewellery and serves as the ornament of fairy royalty. The fairy who first meets Puck, and serves Titania, must 'dew her orbs upon the green' and seek dewdrops in order to 'hang a pearl in every cowslip's ear'. In this world of precious and beneficent water, the destructive flooding caused by the fairy quarrel is all the more striking as an image of disorder. In its ideal form the woodland world of *A Midsummer Night's Dream* is one of sheen, of delicate light on moist surfaces which then seem bejewelled. The moisture in turn suggests, and at last explicitly represents, fertility. In this way the entwined imagery collects ideas which are central to the play within its primary function of atmospheric scene-setting.

The connection with the play's ideas is just as important as the connection with physical action and should deter us from regarding the imagery as merely decorative or lyrical. The bonding of moon with water, and of water with jewels, is meaningful. It links the lunar deity, through the intermediate domain of a liquid, glimmering night landscape, with the Fairy King and Queen, while their natural jewellery in turn links Oberon and Titania with the resplendent monarchic dignity of human rule and power. The associated images suggest an interdependent trinity of powers. Oberon draws on this same pattern of images to suggest the abrogation of proper dignity which Titania's grotesque idolatry of Bottom has produced:

> For she his hairy temples then had rounded
> With coronet of fresh and fragrant flowers.
> And that same dew which sometime on the buds
> Was wont to swell, like round and orient pearls,
> Stood now within the pretty flowerets' eyes
> Like tears . . .
>
> (IV.i.50–55)

Water, jewellery, and the symbols of royalty, and flowers endowed with characteristics analogous to human physical qualities and emotions – all conspire to give the incongruous scene a natural equivalence to human anomaly and disgrace.

Even Caroline Spurgeon is guilty of misreading a speech by elevating the lyrical and picturesque in imagery above its meaningfulness within the play's system of ideas. The above examples of linked imagery of moon, water, flowers and royalty can be set against her comment on a passage from Titania's 'seasons' speech:

We English all know that delightful mid-season of early autumn when the night frosts nip the late summer flowers, and through which the hardy monthly roses persist in gaily blooming, but it is Shakespeare who has painted the poet's picture of it for ever, with its exquisite mingling of sharp air and sweet scents, in the Fairy Queen's description of what was probably the experience of many a gardener at the end of the cold wet summer of 1594:

> . . . we see
> The seasons alter; hoary-headed frosts
> Fall in the fresh lap of the crimson rose,
> And on old Hiems' thin and icy crown
> An odorous chaplet of sweet summer buds
> Is as in mockery set.
>
> (*Shakespeare's Imagery*, pp. 262–3)

It is perfectly true that Shakespeare's seasonal imagery is well-attuned to the delicate transitional points in the yearly cycle, and that in his and other poets' work such moments can be rich in atmospheric suggestion. When T. S. Eliot writes 'Midwinter spring is its own season', readers in

115

Britain and much of North America know exactly what he means, as we know what Nashe means when he writes of 'Back-Winter' in *Summer's Last Will and Testament*. There is a perfect example in Titania's speech, when she speaks of 'the middle summer's spring'. For her it is the time of year which marked the start of Oberon's hooligan incursions into her fairy revels, but in fact it is the precise season of the play itself. The 'middle summer's spring' is the time between May Day and Midsummer's Day, the six weeks or so of early English summer, begun and ended by the two folk festivals between which the play commutes so cavalierly. The season is given precise botanical registration in the play: it includes both the flowering of the cowslips which are Titania's pensioners, and the 'sweet muskroses' and the 'eglantine' which deck the bank where Titania sleeps. The play's scene-setting is faithful in observant detail to an atmospheric phase of English summer.

This is not, however, what Titania is describing in the passage Spurgeon quotes. She is not lyrically celebrating a precise mid-autumn moment, but speaking of extreme seasonal upheaval. The passage follows on immediately from the moon's anger and the inundation of untimely water, and extends the idea to seasonal disturbance. Wintry frost takes flowers of freshening summer, while the god of winter (crowned like a natural monarch) is incongruously enlaurelled with a ring of summer buds. Summer in winter and winter in summer are Titania's evocations, not a Keatsian moment of mid-autumnal change. The difference is that Titania's speech, rescued from lyric ornament, becomes a key statement in the play's concern with the reverberations of disordered love.

Sometimes the play's dominant image patterns are less serious than is commonly supposed, and this is especially true of the many references to animals and wild creatures. Certainly there are suggestions of danger here, audible very late in the play indeed, when Puck's 'wolf behowls the moon'. In general, however, much of the play's animal imagery is comic and reductive, the more so because (like the moon) it is intelligently sophisticated by the artifice of mythology.

As with the moon imagery, the animal imagery has physical theatricality to support it, and again we are much indebted to the mechanicals for this. Before there is any risk of encounters with a real lion in the wood, we have met a most innocent and kindly Lion in the person of Snug the Joiner. Probably we have heard him roaring and been terrified into laughter. A neutralized Lion, deeply anxious not to cause offence, has been comically interposed between the audience and any notion of a troublesome reality. This, of course, has nothing on Bottom as the ass. Oberon has altogether wilder creatures in mind for

Titania to idolize when she awakes; his first prospective repertoire includes the 'lion, bear, or wolf, or bull', the monkey and the ape, with further variations (as he actually anoints her eyes) to include the 'ounce or cat or bear,/Pard, or boar with bristled hair', but what she actually gets is (in literal and metaphoric truth) an ass.

Sinister constructions have been placed on this, most notably by Jan Kott, who observes of Oberon's list of candidates:

All these animals represent abundant sexual potency and some of them play an important part in sexual demonology. Bottom is eventually transformed into an ass. But in this nightmarish summer night, the ass does not symbolize stupidity. Since antiquity and up to the Renaissance the ass was credited with the strongest sexual potency and among all the quadrupeds is supposed to have the longest and hardest phallus.

(*Shakespeare Our Contemporary*, p. 81)

This is a splendidly alarming view of the play's bestiary, but is simply invalidated by the text. The ass is repeatedly cited as a hackneyed metaphor for imbecility, even by Bottom himself ('This is to make an ass of me'). In everything that concerns the mechanicals, literalism of mind is comically at odds with imaginative ambition and uncomprehending failure, and it is one of the play's most delightful reversal-jokes that hackneyed images of ass-like stupidity are reinforced by the physical spectacle of Bottom's transformation, turning the cliché into an improbable literal truth. This most everyday of animal images has gained bizarre and hilarious physical support.

Reversal-jokes of a different kind occur elsewhere, in the chases and disputings of the lovers. When Helena is in fruitless pursuit of Demetrius, he threatens to leave her 'to the mercy of wild beasts', but this unchivalrous withdrawal of masculine protection loses much of its impressiveness because he is not so much deserting Helena as running away from her. The reversal is pointed up (with characteristic intelligence) by Helena herself. She describes herself as his 'spaniel' and invites him to spurn and beat her, but only so that she can dog his heels against his will. Her animal images for their relationship are dominated, however, by those of weak creatures pursuing the strong. Mythology is recruited to support the sense of inversion and artifice in their relationship ('Apollo flies, and Daphne holds the chase'), and mythical beasts are invoked to augment the imaged real ones ('The dove pursues the griffin') so that, when we arrive at beasts which actually exist, they are absorbed into a context of formality and artifice ('the mild hind/ Makes speed to catch the tiger'). This is to say nothing of the improbable

117

presence of any real tigers in a very English wood transposed to Greece. Helena is much addicted to such imagery. A little later she claims to be 'as ugly as a bear', with the same suggestion that her ugliness cancels out defencelessness, so that the gentlest improbably becomes the most fearsome and 'beasts that meet me run away for fear'. The pattern within the imagery is that inversions of accustomed power and status deprive the animal world of its accustomed symbolic associations.

Even the potent image of the serpent is subject to some demotion and ridicule in *A Midsummer Night's Dream*. Hermia, at the end of Act II scene ii, awakes from the play's one literal dream (or nightmare) with frightening dream-images of the serpent at her breast. This image, like Kott's ass, is subject to phallic interpretations for those who find them convincing, but the most powerful dramatic point within the dream is Lysander's indifference, nightmarishly confirmed for Hermia as she awakes to his desertion. It is sexual rejection that Hermia suffers, not sexual attack, and Lysander is more serpentine than the snake of her dream. Similarly, in a passage discussed elsewhere (III.ii.71–3), Hermia accuses Demetrius of lethal treachery to outdo the serpent's, and in the process demotes creaturely violence below human capability. The serpent appears again in a reductive context during the lovers' climactic quarrel in the same scene, when Demetrius and Lysander are attempting to retire for their manly duel over Helena, and Lysander is physically restrained by Hermia. Attempting to shake her off, he threatens that 'I will shake thee from me like a serpent'. Again the image joins with physical theatricality to produce dramatic effect: the coiling evil of the serpent is turned to comic absurdity by Lysander's unseemly struggles to get free.

This is not to argue that the animal imagery of *A Midsummer Night's Dream* is wholly comic, wholly contained by artifice, wholly subdued by human actualities. Behind the play is another surrounding world where genuine dangers exist. Puck's wolf really does behowl the moon. But in this, one of the dominant image patterns, comic incongruity is active in the imagery and interposes a protective laughter between the audience and a full awareness of the wood's dark side. The awareness is never *wholly* obscured: dream is partly nightmare, and images of such derangement populate the play. Although there are birds, and in general the birds are images of harmony, music, gentleness and (in the case of the lark) rescuing daylight, there are also the venomous reptiles and beetles against which the fairies seek to charm Titania in the lullaby. Even the birds include the crow and the raven – not all are melodious and peaceful. In a different area of natural imagery, the clarity of starlight can be obscured by fog, when Oberon wishes Demetrius and Lysander to stray from their aggressive rendezvous, and although the purpose is benevolent, the means are both humiliating and alarming. This double effect of protected nightmare is indeed characteristic of the play and is strongly present in almost all of the imagery, most obviously in the disorientating cover of moonlit darkness in itself. Wilson Knight observed, 'The play continually suggests a nightmare terror. It is dark and fearsome. The nights here are "grim-looked" (V.i.167). And yet this atmosphere of gloom and dread is the playground for the purest comedy. Romance and fun interthread our tragedies here' (*The Shakespearean Tempest*, p. 146). It is an apt comment on the cumulative effect of the *Dream*'s imagery.

There is one other matter which deserves consideration alongside the play's imagery, even though it is not usually regarded as an image in itself but rather as a faculty of the body to which imagery is attached. Eyes and eyesight are major subjects in this play. As with the other groups of references considered above, the abstract or imaginative references have physical correlations which place sight in the forefront of stage action. Above all, of course, we are aware of confused figures, deprived of sight's security, making their way through the darkness of the wood – Demetrius and Lysander in the dark fog, or Hermia, who discovers Lysander by hearing because the darkness 'from the eye his function takes' and 'doth impair the seeing sense'. Indeed the sensory displacement of the eye, and its more equal, complex interplay with hearing, is a feature of experience in the wood. It is directly linked in comic effect to the statements of sensory dislocation that come from the mechanicals. Just before Bottom is translated, Quince tells Flute that Pyramus 'goes but to see a noise that he heard', and this is the beginning of Bottom's transformative experience which ends with his waking to declare that 'The eye of man hath not heard, the ear of man hath not seen . . . what my dream was!' The sense of sight has its place, too, in the violent physical comedy of the women's quarrel: Hermia, though so aggravatingly short compared with Helena, is 'not yet so low/But that my nails can reach unto thine eyes'.

Eyesight is the source of much comedy, in fact. 'Whoever loved that loved not at first sight?', the romantic principle which sanctions the sudden, irrational arbitrariness of love, is taken to satiric extremes in the dramatic awakenings of Titania, Demetrius and Lysander, stirred to redirected passions by the love juice. Sudden ardour is in all these cases made farcical by reflex instancy.

Sensory confusion is also suggested by the double role of the eyes, considered elsewhere in this study – the eyes as perceivers of beauty and the eyes as the objects of beauty perceived. Sometimes the ambiguity is carefully preserved. When Helena speaks of Demetrius 'doting on Hermia's eyes' (I.i.230), does she mean 'doting on the sight of Hermia' or 'doting on the sight of Hermia's eyes'? Likewise with Lysander, declaring that the faculty of reason, which has suddenly converted him to love of Helena, 'leads me to your eyes' (II.ii.127). At other times it is explicitly the eyes which are the object and incitement of infatuation. Demetrius was true to Helena, she says, before he 'looked on Hermia's eyne'.

This may all be seen as a varied play on the contest between the senses, the reason and the irrational passions which is such a powerful continuing preoccupation in the play, and it may be argued that the eyes, which are so often 'imaged', are not themselves truly an image. And yet they effectively become so. Eyesight is a shifting, flexible and destabilized symbol for the internal perceptual organ for which no name exists. Figures in the play receive and act upon the sensory data of what might be called 'imaginative sight'. It is a sense for which the eyes themselves are convenient agents and intermediaries, and for which they supply an opportunistic rationalizing function. The sense which is dominant in daylight – the sensory equivalent of reason – is dislodged from its high office in the darkness of the wood. Helena's intuition is quite right, though her vocabulary is insufficient, when she says 'Love looks not with the eyes, but with the mind.' The nature of love itself, as it is expressed in *A Midsummer Night's Dream*, converts the eye from organ of sense to image, and the darkness of the wood is the physical embodiment of its altered status. The 'poet's eye, in a fine frenzy rolling', which figures with misplaced dismissiveness in Theseus' great speech in Act V, is truly the faculty of imaginative sight, and the eye is its metaphor. This concept of imaginative sight, so crucial to the play's oppositions of ideas, will be considered more fully in the next chapter.

6. The Worlds of Day and Night

Oppositions

As the previous discussion has suggested, the symmetry of composition which is so conspicuous a feature of *A Midsummer Night's Dream* extends beyond language, character and dramatic structure to the systematic ordering of ideas. The play is built around a set of opposites, dualities or polarities which play against each other. Pairs are important throughout. There are two pairs of lovers and two pairs of royal personages, with oppositional relationships at different stages of resolution in each pair. There are two locales, Athens and the wood, the first representing an enclosed, confined and courtly space, the second an open, frontierless and rural one. There are the paired opposites of day and night, light and darkness, sun and moon. The natural inhabitants of the contrasted worlds are opposite in bodily form, the Athenian being solidly physical and, in the persons of Bottom and the mechanicals, gross and heavy, and the woodland figures being light and graceful and, in the persons of the smallest fairies, delicate and airy. The Athenians are mortal, the fairies are immortal. Opposed and contrasted pairings are thus as clear as may be, in the setting and the atmosphere of the play, in character-groups and character-relationships. A similar patterning of opposites can be found in the play's more abstract conditions and ideas.

This systematic binary organization can seem too regular, too contrived and over-cerebral, if we look at it purely as a static phenomenon imprinted on the play, and there is certainly no reason to suppose that the young Shakespeare did not get pleasure from his neatness of design. Static, however, is the least appropriate word for *A Midsummer Night's Dream*, as earlier sections of this study have tried to show. The play is continually in motion, and all the pairings are continually changing their relationship or dominance. At some of the most powerful moments in the drama, two worlds briefly meet, or overlap, or just avoid each other. A summer's dawn is common ground between day and night, light and dark, Theseus and Oberon, waking and sleeping, and in the transitory half-light there are glimpses of a twofold truth; so Hermia can say

> Methinks I see these things with parted eye,
> When everything seems double.
>
> (IV.i.188–9)

A more extraordinary and grotesque encounter between two opposed realities is the relationship of Titania and Bottom, a relationship between immortal and mortal, high and low, ethereal and animal, delicate and gross. Within the relationships there is similar mobility and flux, barely traceable in the state of affairs between Theseus and Hippolyta, but not completely non-existent, and very obvious indeed in the quarrel and reconciliation of Oberon and Titania, and the fluctuating passions of the lovers. As their emotions and fidelities are in processes of change, so are their bodies in movement. So omnipresent is the paired activity that the play's few single figures – Egeus, Philostrate, Puck – stand out as oddities, and only Puck takes on the extra transcendental quality of wholly self-contained, autonomous life. Even he takes evident delight in the comic pattern of doubleness. As he collects the lovers for their final dispositions, the arithmetic neatness is a joke to him:

> Yet but three? Come one more,
> Two of both kinds makes up four.
>
> (III.ii.437–8)

As with people, places, times, so with ideas and conditions. In 'East Coker', T. S. Eliot echoed his Tudor ancestor Sir Thomas Elyot, author of the *Boke named the Governour*, in celebrating

> The association of man and woman
> In daunsinge, signifying matrimonie,

and dances to signify matrimony are performed at the end of Act IV for Oberon and Titania and at the end of Act V for the mortal lovers – indeed two dances in this final instance, because the artisans' Bergomask precedes the fairy round. Matrimony – the association of man and woman as two who become one, and yet remain two – is the principal subject of the play. It is also, however, the paradigm of the relationship of pairs, the symbolic condition to which other dualities or polarities aspire. In marriage, opposites combine; they merge to become one thing, one flesh, but they also complement each other in two separate bodies, their creative and joyous antagonism leading to procreation and new life. In addition to all its other felicities, the place of marriage in *A Midsummer Night's Dream* can only be fully understood if it is seen as intellectually pleasing, the most comprehensive mathematical harmonization of two and one.

Nothing else in the play's arrangement of duets can measure up to that, but the play consistently 'marries' opposites and abstractions in comparable ways. Most important of these, perhaps, is the marriage of sleeping and waking. At the end of the play all the mortals go off to lovemaking and sleep, guarded by the wakeful fairies. Before this night of ordered harmony, the previous night of trials in the wood has been marked by a great deal of sleeping. Titania sleeps, Bottom sleeps, all the lovers sleep – Lysander and Hermia sleep twice. Their emergence from these sleeps is usually a switch to instantaneous, charged, traumatic wakefulness, a sudden stroke of passion or bewilderment. The two conditions are diametrically opposed, but somewhere between them is the enigma of the dream. Dream is the child of sleep, but in fact the play has only one sleeping dream, Hermia's at the end of Act II scene ii, and even her dream is symbolic of the state to which she wakes. Everything else that the characters subsequently call a dream is what we, the audience, know to have been a wide-awake experience.

The best extensive discussion of the nature of dream in this play and in Elizabethan thought is David P. Young's (*Something of Great Constancy*, pp. 115–26). He demonstrates the low regard in which dreams were held in the period, and their association with insubstantiality and illusion elsewhere in Shakespeare. Dreams in popular belief were shadowy, misleading and undependable, and to awake from dreaming was to awake from illusion into truth. This is certainly what Theseus thinks when he hears the story of the lovers' recollections, though Hippolyta is much less sure. But the nature of dream in this play is much less simple. Young observes, 'Shakespeare's characteristic practice with something like the dreaming-waking polarity is to question both concepts, turning them against each other until they acquire a paradoxical relationship,' and he notes that it is the stupid Bottom who responds most accurately to his supposed dream experience on waking.

In *A Midsummer Night's Dream*, the characters' dreams are only illusions in the contextual sense that the play which frames them is illusion. In so far as the play is a fiction, and the audience is conscious of theatrical illusion, then the dreams are illusion within an illusion, and the play's title describes the audience's experience; in so far as we provisionally acquiesce through our imagination to the play as 'true', then the dreams of the characters are waking dreams, living experiences, and 'true'. In the end, the truth of dream is inseparable from imagination, art and theatrical 'truth'. The night-time experiences cannot be dismissed *within* the play, as Theseus tries to do, because he is mistaken. They can only be dismissed by references external to the play, and if we do that we risk 'doing a Theseus'. At one level we are ourselves experiencing dramatic illusion, or a waking dream. Like Theseus, the audience can choose between consenting imaginatively to the improbable story we are told or dismissing it as illusion and dream. But the difference between waking and sleeping is a crucial one. Its sharply articulated opposition within the play is therefore a means to open up more searching questions about the nature of dream and 'truth'. In answering questions his play poses, it is arguable that even Shakespeare was not fully in possession of the terms he needed; I shall return to this point later in considering Puck's epilogue. For the moment, this discussion may illustrate the truth of Young's point, that the polarity (which in my view lies between sleeping and waking rather than between dreaming and waking) is the means to open up paradox and intellectual challenge. It creates the space for a different idea of dream – the waking dream, or the dream which embodies a coexistent truth. This idea, situated between the polarities of sleep and waking, questions the established categories and judgements, and denies the limits set by Theseus.

The second of the play's great intellectual polarities is that between reason and imagination. Theseus' famous speech at the beginning of Act V scene i is again the conceptual centrepiece of the play, but in giving it that status it is important not to treat it as an authoritative statement which enjoys some kind of choric dependability external to the play. It is a speech within the play, made by a thoughtful, intelligent and rational character who is nevertheless fallible. Just as his scepticism about the believability of reported 'dreams' is seen to be fallible, because he is under-informed and has not seen what we have, so his more inclusive statement about the respective status of reason and imagination may prove to be both partial and inadequate.

Shakespeare's exploration of the polarities in this play often works from a starting-point where there is some ambivalence in the more contentious of the two opposites. Wakefulness is presumed to be trustworthy and dream illusory, but sleep, the normal habitation of dream, is in itself necessary and good. Likewise reason is presumed to be dependable and estimable. The high eminence of reason in Elizabethan hierarchic thinking is beyond dispute. We have already seen that the lovers try to justify their irrational behaviour by constructing plausible frameworks of reason to support themselves, and even the thick-skin Bottom, when he observes that love and reason keep little company nowadays, is in no doubt that they ought to. There is no question of demoting reason from its earned and justified high status in this contest of polarities, or that Theseus is a commendable figure who defends it.

Rather the question which is raised is whether reason is sufficient in itself to account for all experience, or whether there are parts of life which need other terms of understanding.

Here imagination is in a similar position to that of sleep and dream. In contemporary Elizabethan thinking the status of imagination was lower than that of reason, and its proper place lay within a system of relativities. Imagination is not wrong or undesirable in itself, but undesirable if it displaces reason from its position of primary authority, becoming out of hand, excessive and ungovernable. Pejorative references to imagination (in Shakespeare as elsewhere) are customarily to *uncontrolled* imagination. Allowed unlicensed range beyond the constraints of reason, imagination could liberate interior conditions of disorder, which may then take external forms such as passion, anarchy or madness. Imagination's true place lay in ordered hierarchical subjection to the higher faculty of reason, acting as an intermediary agent between the rational powers and the senses. When Theseus in his great speech sets reason and imagination in opposition to each other, he is not considering them as equals. The unfortunate position of imagination was that it was almost bound to lose in one or other of two ways: either it was too closely tied to the senses, and therefore too prone to sensory distraction from the authority of reason, or it was too free of affiliations either to reason or the senses, and therefore liable to generate illusions by its unconfined activity.

Against this suspect and subordinate placement, however, must be set the powers and qualities that imagination could be allowed. Imagination was not only a receptive agency for the impressions which the senses supplied, but the faculty by which they were stored, arranged and valued. It therefore has several potential roles which endow it with respectability and importance, to set against its junior and potentially disordering relationship with reason. It provides the rational powers with a source of knowledge derived from sensory experience; it has a 'shaping' or 'making' quality which is itself a creative action exerted upon sensory data, and it has autonomous generative capabilities which could be viewed with something less than complete scepticism and distrust. What matters in relation to the thought-patterns of *A Midsummer Night's Dream* is above all the fact that imagination was a concept surrounded by contentious uncertainty and possible contradictions, rather than fixed evaluative judgement.

In Theseus' speech, imagination is set in paired and oppositional relationship to reason, but is also subdivided into subsidiary and constituent relationships. In these the uncertainties described above are clearly detectable. Theseus finds imagination at large in three groups:

> The lunatic, the lover and the poet
> Are of imagination all compact.
>
> (V.i.7–8)

Reason, that is to say, is set in several oppositional pairings under the umbrella of imagination. The pairings are reason and madness, reason and love, reason and poetry. Little analysis is needed to see that these subordinate antitheses make it impossible to give to imagination a single function or meaning or value. Madness is diametrically opposed to reason and true judgement: it is irrational, illusory and false, especially in relation to excess. The madman not only sees devils, but unrealistic numbers of them. The lover ('all as frantic' according to Theseus, but not according to his better-informed audience) sees 'Helen's beauty in a brow of Egypt', and in so doing asserts an alternative perception, a different process of knowing and judging, from the customary one. Love has its own mode of judgement, not easily brought into consonance with the accepted public one and (as we have seen in the case of the lovers) deeply unconvincing when it tries to be so. Down-to-earth Bottom sees at once the absurdity of Titania's passion for him, and tells her so:

... reason and love keep little company together nowadays – the more the pity that some honest neighbours will not make them friends.

(III.i.136–8)

This is not to say that love is inherently and irredeemably irrational, however. Love is capable of a madness of unreason and incongruity *at times*; Titania's contrived adoration of Bottom is a visible and hilarious example of love as a madness, and Lysander's Act I duet with Hermia laments other forms. But love is not incompatible with reason, provided it observes its own internal rationales, and provided that external forces are amenable to the outcome of love's reason.

It is precisely such an achieved compatibility that *A Midsummer Night's Dream* celebrates. Its outcome is marriage, which was discussed in Chapter 2 as an integration of emotive and social, internal and external, measures. The fact of the play's love plot is that love and reason keep little company together in the antics of the love quartet, while they are left to their own devices. For a time, imagination in its form as love seems irretrievably at odds with reason, its madness expressed in volatile, impulsive, irrational behaviour and also in failed efforts to use reason as an aid to self-excuse. This love quartet are in luck, however (in contrast, for example, to Romeo and Juliet): they have honest neighbours to make love and reason friends. One honest neighbour is Oberon, who uses magical powers to correct the subjective irrationalities of passion and restore the symmetrical harmony which existed before Demetrius' madness. The other honest neighbour is Theseus, who intervenes to correct the social irrationality represented by Egeus. With the aid of these two honest neighbours, two and two can make up four.

Theseus knows nothing of Oberon, though, and his analysis is incomplete. It reaches only as far as his own fiefdom of benevolence. Because of our own superior knowledge, we in the audience know that Oberon's role is equal to that of Theseus in achieving the lovers' happiness. Imagination-as-love is therefore vindicated beyond Theseus' power to know it. Imagination and Reason, in the persons of the complementary potentates, are given dramatic equity of status in the achievement of socially acceptable and successful marriages.

The third subordinate pairing is that of reason and poetry. The quality which Theseus perceives in the poet's imagination is different again. It is neither the anarchic destruction of external order which afflicts the madman, nor the operation of a different judgemental function, unstable if devoid of complementary reason, as with the lover, but the autonomous generative faculty which, as set out above, was one of imagination's possible roles. The poet gives shapes to transparencies of air, as indeed the play itself does in its movement from the creative mind to the complex duality of illusion and reality which is stage performance. In speaking of 'airy nothing', Theseus is inadequate. Shakespeare is notable for his ironic preoccupation with the word 'nothing' (above all in *King Lear*) and his cautious refusal to concede the absolute nothingness of 'nothing'. In this speech 'nothing' is Theseus' concept, not Shakespeare's. The process of shaping and naming which Theseus airily dismisses is precisely the creative energy of theatre and of art. Theseus' dismissal of the poet is undercut by his position as an airy nothing given place and name in the play we are watching.

The speech, therefore, contrary to what Theseus 'intends' by it, is a conditional but powerful vindication of imagination's complementary and equal role with reason in the dialectic of understanding. In order to understand it we have to make our own adjustments, prompted by the text, to the way we think about the meaning of 'imagination', just as we did with the meaning of 'dream'. Within the speech we have a further conceptual prompting contained in the words 'apprehend' and 'comprehend'. Designedly, the two words are repeated in conceptual proximity. Apprehension is the province of imagination, comprehension the province of reason. The irrational ones have

> . . . shaping fantasies, that apprehend
> More than cool reason ever comprehends
>
> (V.i.5–6)

and the imagination of these characters plays tricks:

> That if it would but apprehend some joy,
> It comprehends some bringer of that joy.
>
> (V.i.19–20)

David Young observes: 'The difference between "apprehension" and "comprehension" is clear enough here. To comprehend something is to understand it completely. Since intelligibility is impossible in the absence of reason, Theseus has won his case in advance by loading the terms. Apprehension may be a step toward knowledge, but by itself it is unreliable.' He continues a little later: 'Poor Theseus. His reason is overmatched by the facts of the context in which he attempts to exercise it'. Young notes that in the second quotation he mixes up his terminology by allowing imagination to 'comprehend' (*Something of Great Constancy*, pp. 138–9). This seems mainly but not wholly true. 'Comprehension' in this context is most precisely defined not as 'complete understanding' but as 'rational inference'; while 'apprehension' is more accurately defined as 'intuitive perception'. Theseus is not mixing up the meaning of his terms but misapplying their relative values. His seeming confusion about imagination's response to joy consists in supposing that only by rational inference can it be understood. When the imagination is moved by joy, its understanding of a 'bringer' is a function of intelligent perception *in itself*, not of some illusory rational continuum. The effect (contrary to what Theseus is arguing) is to assert the intelligence of imagination in its own right, as a way of knowing which complements reason but does not require to be ratified by it.

Thus Theseus' brilliantly argued error affirms by its confident inadequacies the intellectual structure of the play, which is a celebration of doubleness, of complementary ways of knowing. Their value may lie in mutual necessity and the creative antagonism which exists between them, or in their mergence and fusion. The central event and central image of marriage is both these things. It is surrounded by a set of others, some of which are discussed above: sleep and waking, imagination and reason, art and nature, illusion and truth, licence and order, shadow and substance, the theatre and the world. The clarity of these oppositions allows the play to explore the space between them, to examine the terms themselves and also the intermediate terms which are used, or missing, or needed, or suspectly defined. Between the stasis of the opposites there is ceaseless intellectual mobility. If this sounds cerebral and abstract for a play, we only need to remind ourselves of the dance – the restless mobility of bodies, the vivid physicality of the play; its intellectual design is expressed through means which are wholly theatrical.

The physicality of theatrical expression for the play's intellectual structures is particularly well exemplified by the fact, the image, and the idea of sight and blindness. In the chapter on 'Imagery' we have looked at the prevalence of eye imagery, and its external staging in the spectacle of confused figures searching for each other in the darkness. This is the theatrical language for something which has as its nucleus a double oppositional idea, the two parts of which are joined early in the play by Helena:

> Love looks not with the eyes, but with the mind,
> And therefore is winged Cupid painted blind.
>
> (I.i.234–5)

The conventional mythological figure of blind Cupid is realized in physical actuality throughout the play, in a sensory opposition between the sight of the love object and the blindness of love itself. This sensory image leads logically to the opposition, as Helena expresses it, between ocular and imaginative sight – the dual interactive organs of perception, where imaginative sight is ultimately decisive. The duality enacted here is wholly consistent with the relative positions of imagination and the senses as they were summarized earlier in this chapter, but it implicitly alters the balance of power in the relationship between imagination and reason. Consistent with the enhanced status of imagination, its power to mediate love is granted the title of 'mind'. On the other hand, Helena goes on to deprive this 'mind' of powers of judgement: 'Nor hath love's mind of any judgement taste'. Helena as a character is understandably confused, but Shakespeare is not confused about the conceptual polarities which underlie her speech. Assessed by the criterion of reason, which in orthodox thought is superior to imagination, love is lacking in judgement, but in its autonomous existence as 'mind' it has mysterious intellectual forces of its own. These are unstable, seemingly irrational, yet subject to an inner passionate mentality which has its own forms of order. Except for the vagueness of 'mind', the word to express love's alternative intellect does not exist; but the faculty itself *does* exist, and drives the play.

In the outer sensory image (eyesight) which gives dramatic shape to this idea, the necessary word does indeed exist, but just out of reach. Oberon, instructing Puck on the final treatment of the lovers, says that when the lovers awake from sleep, and Lysander's 'eyeballs roll with wonted sight', all that they have endured will 'seem a dream and fruitless vision'. The words 'dream' and 'vision' may be taken as synonymous, and no significance attached to the detail that it is the *vision* which will *seem* 'fruitless'. Certainly the play does not enforce the distinction, but it comes very close to doing so. Titania, awaking into 'wonted sight' after her affair with Bottom, exclaims 'My Oberon, what visions have I seen!' Bottom himself, awaking from the same strange episode, first declares 'I have had a most rare vision.' After this one use of the word, as he awakens further, he relapses into frequent references to 'dream'. The play is on the very edge of giving 'vision' a qualitative distinction, suggesting transformative experiences of imaginative sight. If so, it is the sensory equivalent of transformative convulsions in love's 'mind'. Once again the network of opposites, sensory and intellectual, has opened up the space for imprecise or nameless processes of mind and passion, which *A Midsummer Night's Dream* lifts up from mere conceptual abstraction and gives, in theatrical terms, 'a local habitation and a name'.

Transformations

Ovid's *Metamorphoses*, a major source for the play, supplied Shakespeare with the story of 'Pyramus and Thisbe' and a number of other items in the mythological background that he drew upon. As we shall see in relation to Act V, these could be half-announced and dependent for their effect on the sophisticated audience's familiarity with Ovid. The translation of *Metamorphoses* into English by Arthur Golding (1567) not only gave Shakespeare his immediate narrative handbook for the stories, but an extended venture in questionable verse-style which he was able to use for comic and satiric effect. Above all, however, *Metamorphoses* gave Shakespeare the central idea of his play, that of metamorphosis itself. The most significant example of metamorphosis in human life is marriage, but the idea of marriage, as we saw in Chapter 2, and of its metamorphic nature, interpenetrates the entire play.

Metamorphosis, or transformation, or change is to be discovered in numerous different forms in the *Dream*, and its opposite is stasis, stillness, changelessness. Throughout this study I have emphasized the importance of movement, and especially of physical movement. Physical stillness (as in sleep) is a powerful complementary effect, and many of the play's most striking moments can be achieved on stage when the convulsive physical activity is arrested. What is true of physical stillness, however, is not true of stillness in its other, more abstract or metaphoric forms. Although the transformative and changeful episodes of the play are diverse in effect – sometimes beautiful and sometimes ugly, natural and unnatural, graceful and grotesque, gradual and sudden – their common opposite of stasis is uniformly treated with an undercutting scepticism.

There is comparatively little suggestion of stasis in the play. (The existence of *pause*, which is conversely so important in its definition of the intervals between betrothal and marriage, and marriage and consummation, is quite different from stasis: it is a measure of reluctant decorum which sets natural temporal rhythms in a state of tension with impatient human will.) Where stasis does occur, then, it merits notice.

The first of its forms is the life of the nun, to which Hermia will be sentenced if she goes on refusing Demetrius. When Theseus speaks to Hermia, and she replies to him, of growing, living and dying in the stillness of virginal seclusion, the natural transformative evolution of a life is portrayed as being artificially denied by the stasis of the nun's vocation. Seeming respect masks actual recoil.

If nun-like steadfastness is one denial of change, the provisional dualities of childhood are another. For a time, as children, the sisterly intimacy of Helena and Hermia was an innocent prefiguration of marriage, the supersessive state of two-becoming-one. Hermia refers to just this process of natural transformation in Act I scene i, when she tells Helena of her plan to meet Lysander 'where often you and I/Upon faint primrose beds were wont to lie', and her 'Farewell, sweet playfellow' is not just a friendly salutation before flight but the final underlining of an outgrown episode of existence. This natural evolution is subject to attempted halting in Act III scene ii, when Helena rebukes Hermia for her supposed disloyalty by reminding her – anachronistically, in the process of human life – of their youthful oneness in untarnished sisterhood. These instances of effortful stasis are discredited by the movement-governed ethic of the play.

This is the context in which I think we should consider one of the play's most enigmatic features, the quarrel between Oberon and Titania for possession of the changeling boy. This character, who never appears, is a troublesome non-presence for interpreters. Is he really an acceptable pretext for such consequential rupturings? What sort of foundation is this for a contention which plunges the fairy kingdom, the seasons and the natural world into ruinous disarray? And even if he is so important, and we can accept that Oberon is not absurdly over-reacting in a childish fit of jealousy, what are we to make of his resulting behaviour towards Titania? Is it not a piece of contemptible bullying and blackmail? What a way to treat your wife! And how irrationally self-defeating, when the chosen method is to lure her into cuckolding you with an ass!

Drawing on Renaissance views of marital relationships, critics have sought to explain and justify Oberon's action as the legitimate exercise of male authority in marriage. On this basis it is not too difficult to reinforce the play's symmetrical structure by drawing a parallel with the relationship of Theseus and Hippolyta. Past antagonism, conflict and male victory lie behind the ducal wedding, and Oberon can be seen as restoring an equivalent male authority by forcibly bringing his own rebellious wife into docile and subordinate conformity. This view of the play is certainly more plausible in historical terms than a pre-feminist depiction of Oberon as a marital thug, but still it does not explain the episode satisfactorily.

In Chapter 2, I argued that the fairy marriage, though closely analogous to human marriage, is not the same: it has its own equivalences and a different sexual convention, consonant with the delicate (and to human eyes inscrutable) balance of order and disorder in the natural world. The changeling boy is surely part of this. The child is indeed a changeling, a mortal, and his mother 'being mortal, of that boy did die'. The rules prescribed by immortality for the fairy powers, and by regular cyclical mutation for the natural world, do not apply to mortal children, even those transposed as changelings. They are born, and change, and grow. Titania's beautiful aria about the pregnant votaress is a claim to possession of the child, but a *temporary* possession by virtue of the very rules of mortality that engendered him. The state of affairs between them is concisely summarized by Puck:

> She never had so sweet a changeling,
> And jealous Oberon would have the child
> Knight of his train, to trace the forests wild.
> But she perforce withholds the lovèd boy,
> Crowns him with flowers, and makes him all her joy.
>
> (II.i.23–7)

Much later in the play and with more evident grotesqueness, Titania will crown Bottom with flowers – but the point is essentially the same. Titania is behaving inappropriately in terms of time and natural being. She is seeking to hold the changeling boy in stasis, perpetuating the decorative infancy which graces both her sense of his sweetness and the celibate memory of his mother. It is a challenge to the principle of growth and mutability in a human child, the Shakespearean offence (most powerfully articulated in *The Winter's Tale*) of seeking to hold time frozen in innocence, stilled in its tracks. Oberon, in seeking possession of the child, is seeking to exercise the quasi-paternal authority which supplants (or, measured by Titania's immortalized femaleness, usurps) the maternal role in the growing, living and dying of a mortal boy. In trying to frustrate the natural transformative sequence of the child's growth, Titania causes comparable unheavals elsewhere: a divorce and pseudo-stasis in her relationship with Oberon, and a disturbance in the natural cycle of weather, seasons and lunar activity. Delighting in one metamorphosis, and seeking to memorialize it through the child, she has interrupted and delayed another.

The changeling child episode among the fairies is a type of the future experience which awaits the three pairs of lovers: marriage, pregnancy, parenthood and the growth of children. Reaching back through the play's recall of their early lives, we first meet them at the earlier stages, when they themselves were children and formed childhood friendships which then turned away to sexual love and courtship, courtship to marriage. The cycle is completely present in the play's imagining. The process of mutation, transformation, metamorphosis is natural and regular. In the external world its counterpart is the regularity of the lunar cycle with which the play begins, and the regularity of day and night, and the regularity of the seasons.

Life is made up of mutation, and human life of mutability. Nothing, save unhealthily, stays still. But metamorphosis as a condition of existence is itself unstable and irregular, vulnerable to sudden and aberrant transformations. Although it is not true to say that sudden transformation is invariably aberrant (the corrective suddenness of Demetrius' restored passion for Helena, and Lysander's for Hermia, are restorations of the natural), it is broadly true to say that gradualness is the typical process of natural metamorphosis, and arbitrary suddenness of unnatural transformation. The vocabulary of love in the play makes the distinction clear. 'Dotage' is the condition of instantaneous, unreasoning and unstable love, and the play is full of people transformed unpredictably into such a state. Love is the name of the *true* condition, distinguishable from reason but governed by its own mysterious rationality, which is trustworthy and the appropriate prelude to enduring marriage. Its eminent quality is, to use C. L. Barber's admirable term, 'clarification', and this is the achieved condition (rather than any significant individual character development) which marks the lovers in

Act V as securely different from their former selves. Dotage, by contrast, is accompanied by confusion. If there is a single point in the text where the distinction is explicit, it is newly-awakened Demetrius' speech to Theseus when the sleeping lovers are discovered (IV.i.159–75). An actor can use it to individualize Demetrius, but the speech's representative quality is what matters. His metamorphosed self, infatuated with Hermia for a time, seems now 'As the *remembrance* of an idle gaud/Which in my *childhood* I did *dote* upon'. Metamorphosis is characterized throughout by the prompt transposition of experience into memory, itself a thing fantastic and recessive, while Demetrius' corrected self in love with Helena is marked by a cumulative style suggesting continuity and constancy.

The play's vocabulary of metamorphosis is distinctive – 'translate', 'transpose', 'transfigure' – but the third of these is different from the others. It is employed by Hippolyta in V.i.24, as she replies to Theseus' scepticism by remarking the cogency of 'all their minds transfigured so together'. 'Translate' and 'transpose' refer to lateral aberrations, detached from suggestions of value, but 'transfigured' suggests an event devoid of *knowable* value, but not of value itself.

As with the oppositions which compose the intellectual system of the play, so transformation has its potent physical expression – nothing more so. Lateral aberration is before us in the comic, grotesque, absurd, hilarious and monstrous person of Bottom the ass. Unnatural transformation is visible and audible, in extreme form, and its absurd results quite beautifully rendered in Titania's paradoxical state of autocratic servitude. The two great scenes of this affair are all the funnier because neither party is wholly changed. Bottom is still Bottom, attractively armed with courteous good sense but wonderfully incapable of being other than he truly is. Titania is still Titania, imperious and dictatorial in her infatuation. Through all the comedy, they make physical the drama's metaphoric 'thesis': in false or insane metamorphosis, the self is deviant and uncontrolled, an aberrant version of its nature; in true metamorphosis, the real self develops. And in keeping with a play of non-psychological procedures, metamorphic development is not primarily expressed in character evolution, but ritualistically in dance, in patterning, and in marriage.

7. The Return to Athens

In Jane Austen's *Northanger Abbey*, the heroine, Catherine Morland, is addicted to Gothic romances, which feature lurid plots depicting the awful fate of heroines. The novel's satiric comedy is consistently directed at Catherine's naïve imaginings and her ability to construct sinister meanings from trivial evidence. Then, near the end of the novel, the tables are suddenly turned on the sophisticated reader. While Catherine is staying at Northanger Abbey, the home of her lover, Henry Tilney, his snobbishly intemperate father discovers Catherine's modest social origins and summarily evicts her from his house. She is left to travel home, in a public conveyance, on her own. To us this may not seem the worst of melodramatic fates that could befall, but in Jane Austen's strict and quiet bourgeois England it is bad enough, and proof that whilst great houses may not be full of mad, imprisoned wives, they are at least capable of unlooked-for social violence. The dangerous world is not entirely a literary convention.

Something of this same effect occurs in Act V of *A Midsummer Night's Dream*. Catherine Morland's ordeal occurs just when her final happiness is fast approaching (and eventually it does arrive). Similarly, the last act of the *Dream* is the climax of achieved happiness, the safest and most confident episode of the play, the immediate prelude to a wedding night and a future of love and promise. With the interlude of the play-within-a-play, the action is full of laughter and merriment shared between the audience-on-stage and the audience in the theatre, a concurrence of actual and anticipated pleasure. This is the festive courtly aftermath to all the tribulations of the wood and the night.

As Jane Austen was to do many years later, Shakespeare elects to turn the tables on us just when he enhances the pitch of comedy. Catherine Morland's happiness, and our happiness in hers, are all the greater because we have been made aware of genuine perils at the edge. So it is with *A Midsummer Night's Dream*, which enhances our pleasure in comedy and joy with a succession of glimpses into other truths, other worlds, other possible outcomes. The more educated and sophisticated the audience, the more there are that will be noticed – reminders of mortality are everywhere in this concluding act. They do not in any sense weaken the comedy, but they shape it. Anne Barton has set out quite admirably both the doubleness of tone in this part of the play, and the effect it should have in the theatre:

Without meaning to do so, Bottom and his associates transform tragedy into farce before our eyes, converting that litany of true love crossed which was rehearsed in the very first scene by Hermia and Lysander into laughter. In doing so, they recapitulate the development of *A Midsummer Night's Dream* as a whole, re-enacting its movement from potential calamity to an ending in which quick bright things come not to confusion, as once seemed so inevitable, but to joy. An intelligent director can and should ensure that the on-stage audience demonstrates some awareness of the ground-base of mortality sounding underneath the hilarity generated by Bottom's performance, that a line like Lysander's 'He is dead, he is nothing . . .' is not lost in the merriment.

Introduction to the play in
The Riverside Shakespeare, 1974

At risk of seeming to solemnize the glorious farce of 'Pyramus and Thisbe', in the following discussion I shall try to show the undertones of mortality, and of catastrophic alternatives in love, which underlie and sharpen the fun and merriment of the scene.

They begin with Theseus' choice of play, from the eccentric menu given by Philostrate. Even the least sophisticated audience will agree with Theseus that the offerings he rejects are non-starters, dealing as they plainly do with war, violence and poverty. Not one of them is 'sorting with a nuptial ceremony'. For an audience familiar with its myths, and more particularly with Ovid's *Metamorphoses*, there is rather more to it than that. The first potential entertainment is *The Battle with the Centaurs*, 'to be sung/By an Athenian eunuch to the harp'. Theseus gives summary judgement – 'We'll none of that' – and well he might, not only because a eunuch might be a figure of incongruous pathos on a wedding night. In Ovid, the battle with the Centaurs was an event in which Theseus was himself involved. And at a wedding feast, of all things.

In Book XII of *Metamorphoses* a marriage is arranged between Pirothous, son of Ixion, and the beautiful Hippodame. Theseus was present at the marriage feast along with all the 'Lordes of Thessaly', and so were the fierce cloud-born centaurs. When Hippodame made her impressive entry, the epitome of beauty, she unfortunately provoked the wine-heated passions of Eurytus, cruellest of all the centaurs, who seized the bride by the hair to carry her off. Theseus himself was nobly prompt in springing to her defence, and the unseemly consequences are graphically described by Arthur Golding in the translation Shakespeare knew:

> And first sayd Theseus thus: What aylst? art mad, O Eurytus?
> That darest (seeing me alive) misuse Pirothous?
> Not knowing that in one thou doost abuse us both? And least
> He myght have seemed to speake in vayne, he thrust way such as preast
> About the bryde, and tooke her from them freating sore thereat.
> No answere made him Eurytus (for such a deede as that
> Defended could not bee with woordes) but with his sawcye fist
> He flew at gentle Theseus face, and bobd him on the brist.
> By chaunce hard by, an auncient cuppe of image woork did stand,
> Which being huge, himself more huge Sir Theseus tooke in hand,
> And threw't at Ewryts head. He spewd as well at mouth as wound
> Mixt cloddes of blood, and brayne and wyne, and on the soyled ground
> Lay sprawling bolt upryght.
>
> (*Metamorphoses*, XII, 256–68)

No wonder Theseus did not fancy a replay of these bloody doings at his own most gracious marriage.

The next on the list is not much better, though Theseus is spared embarrassing mementoes of his personal history. '*The riot of the tipsy Bacchanals,/Tearing the Thracian singer in their rage*' is a reference to Ovid's account of the poet Orpheus' death at the hands of the maddened Ciceronian women, one of whom (in Golding) began the slaughter thus:

> Beholde (sayes shee) behold yoon same is he that doth disdeine
> Us women. And with that same woord shee sent her lawnce amayne
> At Orphye's singing mouth.
>
> (*Metamorphoses*, XI, 6–8)

This too is inappropriate wedding fare. Its example of violent relations between male and female is as tuneless as could be with the harmonies of a wedding night, so Theseus spurns it on the excuse that it is theatrical old hat. In the many-layered comedy of this scene we are shortly to be treated to another example of theatrical old hat: the antiquated style of 'Pyramus and Thisbe' would have seemed quaint and hilarious to the newly sophisticated theatre audience of the 1590s. Nor would such an audience have been unresponsive to the hinted self-mockery of the poet-dramatist, invoking the sanguinary image of a dismembered poet to an audience at whose mercy his own offering would shortly lie.

The third of Peter Quince's competitors, the 'satire keen and critical' on the death of learning, is a hit at ill-timed theatrical pedantry and is quickly seen off. What all three of the discarded entertainments share with 'Pyramus and Thisbe', however, is the event of death. Whichever option Theseus chose for his nuptial evening, he was fated to be shown a corpse. For the educated audience, able to pick up the references, the incongruities are very funny, but only as a *memento mori* is sardonically funny when you are young and fit.

The hilarious bloodshed of 'Pyramus and Thisbe' needs no demonstrating, but Quince's text has further part-concealed black borders in its comedy. These are concentrated in the love duet between Pyramus and Thisbe themselves (V.i.191–200), an exchange which is a comic echo of the Act I love duet between Lysander and Hermia, and helps to remind the real-life audience that these urbane spectators of Quince's play were recently in similar plight themselves. Their happy emergence is delightful but not inevitable, and Bottom and Flute have contrary instances to show. Limander and Helen, in the mechanicals' tortuous mythology, are presumably Leander and Hero, whose illicit love is depicted in Marlowe's poem and who came to a bad end, but the mixed-up names also suggest Alexander (or Paris) and Helen, whose adulterous affair precipitated the fall of Troy. The other lovers, Shafalus and Procrus, are again Ovidian in source: in the *Metamorphoses* (Book VII) they are Cephalus and Procris. Although these lovers enjoyed many years of contented marriage, their relationship began and ended disastrously. At the beginning the disguised Cephalus, misled by a jealous goddess, contrived to seduce his own wife, and ultimately, in a tragic accident caused by her mistaken jealousy of him, he killed her.

The theatrical contrivance is clear enough. In the story of 'Pyramus and Thisbe' itself, and in its rivals for performance, and in its own rhetorical detail, tales and instances of violence, misfortune, jealousy and death in the affairs of love are made hilarious by circumstance, or style, or manner of performance. But in every case the laughter has an outer rim of catastrophe to remind all audiences, both fictional and real, that present happiness is not a rule of life. Awareness of the outer rim is then intensified by Puck's 'Now the hungry lion roars . . .' There are genuine lions in the world as well as Snug the Joiner. Puck's great speech articulates the dangers, even though he places them outside a magically protected circle of safety.

We are not yet finished with comic metamorphosis in Act V; nor is it confined to the play-within-a-play. Although the lovers' transformations are now over, there is further evidence of human instability, and in the most unlikely quarter. Theseus and Hippolyta have been the stablest persons of the play, and their balanced speeches have combined to form some complementary truths, as we saw in the opening lines of the play. At this late stage of events it is timely to remember these. More recent encounters with Theseus and Hippolyta, in Act V itself, showed us Theseus as the rational questioner of imagination's powers, while Hippolyta found something in the lovers' unison of memory which 'More witnesseth than fancy's images'. More recently still, when 'Pyramus and Thisbe' was chosen as the evening's play and Theseus overruled Philostrate's derogatory verdict on it, Hippolyta was the one who showed compunction at the prospect of having to watch the mechanicals' ham-fisted and ham-acted zeal. Once the play is begun, however, we find that these positions are arbitrarily transposed. Theseus, that recent disparager of imagination, is now its defender and Hippolyta, so recently solicitous for the endangered dignity of these hapless Athenians, is now intolerant of them:

> HIPPOLYTA   This is the silliest stuff that ever I heard.
> THESEUS   The best in this kind are but shadows; and the worst are no worse, if imagination amend them.
> HIPPOLYTA   It must be your imagination, then, and not theirs.
>
> (V.i.207–11)

Hippolyta has become brusquely dismissive, Theseus understanding and indulgent, a reversal of their attitudes earlier in the scene. As Quince's play progresses we come across another comic reversal of attitudes, but to notice it we must stretch further back in memory to those same opening speeches of the play. The very first thing we heard was Theseus' impatient complaint about the slow, unhastenable regularity of the lunar cycle and its temporal impediment to their coming marriage, while Hippolyta responded with assurances that the moon's regularity would seem swift. Unchangeable natural evolutions were subject to the relativities of human perception, with Theseus being the impatient one. Now, as they watch poor Starveling impersonating Moonshine, things are otherwise:

> HIPPOLYTA   I am aweary of the moon. Would he would change.
> THESEUS   It appears by his small light of discretion that he is in the wane. But yet in courtesy, in all reason, we must stay the time.
>
> (V.i.244–8)

Perhaps Hippolyta is abashed by this gentle husbandly reproof and is conceding his point a few lines later when she says 'Truly, the moon shines with a good grace', but most actresses will find that a tone of resigned sarcasm comes more easily. Certainly her impatience has not gone when Thisbe arrives and discovers her bereavement: 'I hope she will be brief.'

As comic transformations and reversals go in *A Midsummer Night's Dream* this is a very minor and untroubling example, but it shows that the process has not been halted by a wedding night. To the very last, the relationship between Theseus and Hippolyta contains signals of mutual conflict within harmony. And the manner of Theseus' good-humoured reproof deserves our notice. Not only does he insist on observance of time's decorum, as the marriage ritual has throughout, but he does so with the two terms that have come to represent both his strengths and his limitations. To behave by 'all reason' is the Duke's measure in all things, and as an ethical positive in the play it is admirable in itself, limited only by its lack of access to imaginative knowledge which the real-life audience has been entrusted with. Courtesy, too, is the Duke's great strength throughout, and, as we saw earlier, a failure of courtesy was a noticeable shortcoming in the lovers. Perhaps the aristocratic courtesy of the ducal audience is not impeccably observed as they watch the mechanicals, but its status as a courtly ideal is unquestioned. The ethics of the play are alive in the responses of the on-stage audience, and the minor comic reversal of the roles of Theseus and Hippolyta is intermeshed with all that has gone before.

The reversal of these two roles, in their attitude towards imagination and the mechanicals' play, serves a dramatic purpose in orchestrating the effects of this final scene. At the beginning of the act the attitudes of Theseus to 'the lunatic, the lover and the poet' must be seen as partial and inadequate, and the effect is to demote the place of reason as the sole criterion by which the life of love and imagination can be judged. As the centre of gravity moves from love's truth to theatre's truth, so Theseus' status needs to be again enhanced. No longer is he the intelligent, rational but under-informed judicial voice. Instead he is the senior benevolent presence in the on-stage audience, the closest dependable mediator for the real-life audience to identify with. Although before the play ends there will again be a significant discrepancy between what Theseus sees and what the real-life audience sees, this time it will be a different one. We see Theseus behaving for the most part very well in the mechanicals' scene, only to be finally caught in an Austenesque trap: in the end his rationality is overtaken by unexpected imaginative truth. When the entertainment ends and the courtly figures leave the stage, we are briefly distanced from Theseus. Once again we are complacent possessors of superior knowledge: we see the fairies move in. But if the close of the play is well managed, its very last effect is to cast us all, the real-life audience, as Theseus-like persons, with the vital difference that *we* are made aware of it. All this complexity of effect, of changing relationships with the audience-on-stage, depends on the role of Theseus. He is noble and admirable, yet there are important truths that he does not know and never finds out.

The cue for a way to read this final episode of the play is given by John Russell Brown:

If one wished to describe the judgement which informs *A Midsummer Night's Dream*, one might do so very simply: the play suggests that lovers, like lunatics, poets, and actors, have their own 'truth' which is established as they see the beauty of their beloved, and that they are confident in this truth for, although it seems the 'silliest stuff' to an outsider, to them it is quite reasonable; it also suggests that lovers, like actors, need, and sometimes ask for, our belief, and that this belief can only be given if we have the generosity and imagination to think 'no worse of them than they of themselves'.

(*Shakespeare and his Comedies*, p. 90)

Not only does this repeat the important truth that there are correspondences between the love plot of the middle scenes and the theatrical entertainment of the last act, but it links both to questions of imagination and consenting belief. In a sense the whole play of *A Midsummer Night's Dream* is dealing with those questions of audience response and approval, of imaginative acquiescence, suspension of disbelief and willingness to be entertained, which are the subject of mock-apologetic and ingratiating epilogues to so many other plays. Conventionally, the major character, or actor-as-character, stands forth at the end to regret the play's shortcomings, promise to do better next time, and beg nevertheless for a final round of applause. The best and most interesting of such apologists are those who have themselves played a character-as-director role in the play we have seen – Rosalind in *As You Like It*, Prospero in *The Tempest*. In *A Midsummer Night's Dream* it is finally to be Puck (another character-as-director), but the effect is more complicated.

Before that greatest of reversal-epilogues, however, we have gone through a whole sequence of prior, intermediate stages. At the beginning of Act V, as he talks with Hippolyta about the lovers' strange experiences, the role of Theseus is that of audience – an audience for magic, imagination and love. We too, in the theatre, have been an audience for these events and know them to be 'true'. That is, while knowing they are the stuff of a play and therefore illusory, we have consented imaginatively to their truthfulness through the power of the dramatist's art. Therefore

141

we know that Theseus is wrong in his dismissiveness, and that reason does not measure everything.

In the last act, the fictiveness of theatre is brought on stage twice over, as we watch a play about people watching a play. Its comic self-reflexive intricacy is well described by M. C. Bradbrook:

The mechanicals' play apes the flight from Athens, though of course the parallel is not visible either to them or to their highly condescending auditory: it is part of the 'mirror' technique of the play-within-the-play, where Bottom so laboriously makes everyone comfortable with explanations of the difference between life and art, and where the fun puts both players and audience together inside the jest of professional actors pretending to be mechanicals trying to be amateur actors before an unreal audience. There is a special pleasure in this play within the play from the actors' point of view . . .

(*Shakespeare and Elizabethan Poetry*, p. 157)

This time our relationship with the stage experience is much more complicated and is coloured by our earlier imaginative assent to the dramatic fantasy of the love scenes. We have already accepted the presence of a truth in events which we know to be, strictly speaking, untrue; this affects the way we watch 'Pyramus and Thisbe'. Much of its entertainment value is direct and straightforward. The ludicrous absurdity of the performance works quite simply, and in laughing at it we are sharing the reactions of the on-stage audience, seeing what they see, using them as a transparent filter for our own entertainment, or even bypassing them altogether. When the style of 'Pyramus and Thisbe' parodies old-fashioned plays, the result is funny; when the actors get their lines wrong and their punctuation wrong, we find that funny too – there are many parts of this grotesque farce that we can watch with no intermediate help at all. The conversion of tragedy into farce is amusing in its incongruity for all audiences, fictive or real, at all times.

Other elements of our response, however, depend on factors that we interpose between ourselves and the on-stage audience. When these young, newly-married lovers laugh at Moonshine, we recall seeing them in confused humiliation in the moonlight; when they laugh at Lion, we recall their own concern with dangers from wild beasts; when they do indeed discover 'tragical mirth' in the deaths of Pyramus and Thisbe, we know that they have been lucky to escape a similar fate. If we have read our Ovid we also know that Pyramus and Thisbe (like Romeo and Juliet) were destroyed by a secret love which defied parental disapproval, and we remember the defeated tyranny of Egeus. This courtly audience, now so pleased with itself, would be laughing on the other side of its face if it knew what we know.

In our reactions to the play-within-a-play and to the on-stage audience, it is especially the collapse of imagination that we notice. Bottom and company are incorrigibly literalist. They do not know what imagination is. Nobody could find fault with Starveling for his exasperated quitting of script and role in order to tell the audience directly about his person as Moonshine: the poor man has been sorely tried by witty heckling courtiers. He tells them all the details of his lunar impersonation as if they were literally true, and who can blame him? Bottom also emerges from his part, to thwart Theseus' modernistic exercise in plot-prediction by insisting on the authority of his text, and who can blame him either? Any surviving remnants of dramatic illusion are destroyed by the prudent business of self-naming which the actors have been planning for so long. There can never have been actors more ambitious than Bottom or less ambitious than his friends, yet their ill-assorted pretensions are comically equal in imaginative failure. In the same way, the most inflated language of their play remains leadenly earthbound. The opportunities for real-life actors are superb.

The audience-on-stage responds with witty comments on this benighted literalism, treating like with like. When Theseus suggests that Wall should answer back to Pyramus' curses, he is being literalist and reasonable in order to tease the mechanicals for their literalism, and the other courtiers take their cue from him. Their heckling repartee has its climax in the literalist exchange about the properties of the man in the moon, which so upsets Starveling. Theseus may have recommended the audience-precept of imaginative amendment, but he does not practise what he preached. The temptations of wit and reason are too strong for all the audience-on-stage, and override imagination.

But the real-life audience is differently placed, educated by the prior action to value imagination at more than its customary rate. The ideas which are active in *A Midsummer Night's Dream* (discussed in the previous chapter) serve to create this frame of mind as we watch the closing scenes. Therefore we are doubly entertained by imaginative failure: by that of the mechanicals, but also – despite our amused connivance with their literalist teasing – by that of the on-stage audience too.

Even so, Theseus has taught us how to watch a play, and found words for the reciprocal creation of theatrical magic which the life of the whole play endorses. 'The best in this kind are but shadows; and the worst are no worse, if imagination amend them.' At the end of a conventional play, this will be our magnanimous reaction to the epilogue. In a few moments more we shall be ourselves again, making our way home through the streets, in the real world. We shall be fully aware that it was a play we were so recently watching, that it was not factually 'true', that it was composed of pretences by imperfect actors. We shall know that we collaborated with the actors through a process of willing, self-forgetful imagination to believe in a transitory fictional 'truth' which entertained us, and is now left behind. The advice that Theseus gives is not only generous and courteous but, in its way, self-interested. Theatrical imagination allows us to enjoy ourselves. It is not incompatible with reason or with the authority of literal truth, which resume their accustomed government of our minds as soon as the play is over. The conventional epilogue is underpinned by these very same assumptions.

To appreciate the originality, and the adventurousness, of *A Midsummer Night's Dream*, we have to accept that Puck's epilogue is different. Not only is it different in itself, but its effect is enhanced because so many elements of the conventional epilogue have already anticipated it, incorporated in the events of the play. Usually, the speaker of the epilogue is the first to step outside the contractual bounds of dramatic illusion, announce his or her identity as actor as well as character, and place us self-consciously in our role as audience, on trial for this test of our goodwill. In *A Midsummer Night's Dream* this last self-consciousness as an audience, returning from our voluntary conspiracy in dramatic illusion, has actually been our situation ever since the return to Athens – and also, in subtler ways, even earlier than that. This allows Puck's epilogue to achieve the most extraordinary of double effects – to give a powerful warranty for the 'truth' of dramatic illusion, and the partial illusoriness of conventional extra-dramatic 'truth'. *A Midsummer Night's Dream* challenges us to take the truth of reason and the truth of imagination, the truth of waking and the truth of dream, the truth of Theseus and the truth of Oberon, as complementary realities, and to occupy for a moment as we leave the theatre exactly that transient moment of visionary perception that the lovers, and then Bottom, experienced when they awoke to the daylight of the forest morning. This effect is only achievable because Act V is so triumphantly a play of audiences, and because the whole play to which we have imaginatively assented has so marvellously succeeded in dissociating dreams from sleep.

As we have seen, the detachment of dreamlike experience from literal sleeping is largely accomplished in the first phase of the play, during the night-time transformations of the wood. Even Hermia's nightmare is so exact a corollary with events that it seems a symbol or half-knowledge of the peril she awakes to. With this one exception, the play seems bent on affirming that wakefulness is just as much the province of dream, or dreamlike vision, as sleep itself is. It is when the characters are awake that their experience is dreamlike or perceived as dream. Even the effects of the magic love juice are not preceded (as they might quite plausibly have been) by any sleep-anticipations of the transformations that they cause. In the wood, sleep is mostly a respite from disturbing dream-experience rather than the precondition of it. As he plots the lovers' and Titania's awakening, Oberon is twice at some pains to make it clear that dream is what his transformed clientèle will *think* their night experiences were made of, rather than the waking episodes which they actually were. The lovers' confusions 'Shall *seem* a dream and fruitless vision', and we 'know' imaginatively that in ascribing them to dreaming the lovers will be mistaken.

Sure enough, this is exactly what they do. Whether as dream or vision, the sleepers awakening see their night experiences as something other than the daylight truth, though all of them occupy a momentary half-light of transfiguring recall. For Titania, Bottom and the lovers alike, events are so contrived that they end the night in dreamless sleep, which makes it all the easier for them, when they wake up, to explain their memory by defining it as dream. As an audience we know otherwise, and the ambiguous status of dreamlike truth within wakefulness is implanted in our own perception. Bottom, on waking, becomes within minutes virtually his own audience, his 'dream' transposed into Peter Quince's ballad, and the lovers spontaneously form themselves into a group audience for their own dreamings. Their rationale of waking disbelief is thus distinguished from our own consent to the truths we have seen them undergo.

Armed with this theatrical intelligence, we next see them as the audience for a comically inadequate play. One feature of 'Pyramus and Thisbe' is that it repeatedly enacts the functions of a dramatic epilogue. Quince's Prologue is an epilogue in advance, apologizing for the play's inadequacies and hoping not to cause offence. Theatrical apologia is made the object of theatrical merriment. It is going to be hard to take apologetic afterwords at all seriously in the wake of Quince. Likewise the epilogue's professional address, with character and actor inseparably self-presenting, is comically foreshadowed in the self-announcements of Snout and Snug – combinations of actor and part of such exaggerated unlikelihood that they incite hilarity and pathos. It is foreshadowed also by Snug's prudent anxiety to appease potential audience displeasure. Actor and part come even more unstitched in the impromptu self-assertions of Bottom and Starveling. In a successful play the epilogue marks the formal recession of the play's imaginative world. 'Pyramus and Thisbe', having no imaginative world to recede from, collects bits and pieces of epilogue technique as it goes along. The mechanicals' play, and the on-stage responses to it, thus steal one of the real-life audience's roles, and pre-empt the possibility of a conventional epilogue.

Similarly, the usual end-of-play resumption of reason's authority (in intellectual distinction from imagination) is made harder by the 'thinking' of the mechanicals, and the parodic reaction to it by the on-stage audience. Literalism itself becomes a parody of reason and a comic limitation of possible 'truth'. The words 'true' and 'truth' occur frequently in 'Pyramus and Thisbe', sometimes as a convenient word-plug or phrase-filler for their clumsy scansion, sometimes as a ludicrous claim to verisimilitude. Somewhere or other there is a 'truth' that plays might achieve, but this one gets nowhere near it. Comic literalism is the feeble substitute, and it is on this level that their clever audience responds. But clever audiences can be caught out: when Demetrius scoffs at reason and literalism, saying that one lion may speak 'when many asses do', and when Theseus declares that Bottom as Pyramus may well recover 'and prove an ass', their wit is overridden for the real-life audience by memories of another ass, ridiculous and wonderful, whom the Queen of the Fairies loved. As we watch this foolish play, we can enjoy our response of reasoned wit which colludes with the on-stage audience, but as we watch the *whole* play, in which the courtiers too are actors, imagination takes precedence over reason.

By the time the courtiers go off to bed, therefore, we have already been prepared for something extraordinary. Many of our usual end-of-play responses have been borrowed and incorporated in the play itself. Bereft of our usual audience manners, what are we going to do? The usurpation of our end-of-play role is completed by Theseus, when Bottom offers him the option of an epilogue or a dance: 'No epilogue, I pray you; for your play needs no excuse.' If there is a genuine epilogue after that, it will not be an ordinary one; and who is qualified to speak it? Not Bottom, not Theseus. Not Athens. In his speech to Bottom, Theseus maintains to the end his balanced role as an on-stage audience of whom we can approve. He is amusedly (and truthfully) condescending about the quality of the play, but he is also scrupulously generous and courteous to the actors. As a character he is an exemplary role-model for sophisticated audiences. As an actor, he stands, at one remove, for the apologetic actor in the normal epilogue, and gives alternative advice: 'let your epilogue alone'. Actor, character and audience at once, he has borrowed all our clothes. Where does that leave us? It leaves us with his own choice – a dance, the mechanicals' Bergomask. Many plays end with a dance.

But this play is not over. When the Bergomask is finished, all the courtiers on stage – our own representatives – troop off to bed. For as Theseus says, '`tis almost fairy time'. He does not expect *real* fairies, of course; it is a throwaway conventional metaphor, and perhaps a final teasing joke at the lovers' fancies.

As soon as he has gone, and the coast is clear, 'Enter Puck'. We have heard flippant courtly jokes about asses, but seen (in wonderful completeness) an ass. We have heard experiences dismissed as dreams, but seen their waking truth. We have heard peripheral literary echoes of ill-fated love, but seen its fortunate evasion. We have seen a travesty of the moon, but seen in our imagination the moon itself. Now we hear Theseus' casual witty reference to fairies, and behold! the fairies are there, invading the protected world of Athens, court and audience. And first there is Puck.

If shadows of misfortune and mortality have lain at the edges of the last act's farcical delight, now they come to the fore in Puck's great speech. This is the world of real lions, not Snug; of real death, not Pyramus; of real ghosts and restless spirits, 'spirits of another sort' for Oberon and Puck; of the moon that not only cares for chastity and rules the tides, but calls the wild into nocturnal life. This is the alternative world that lies far outside the perimeter of reasoning Theseus and his palace, in a wider circle that is outside even Oberon and Puck.

Puck is two beings here: he is the domestic sprite and the mystery. He is the incantatory summoner of the truths of darkness, but also the free servant and protector of human safety. His voice, unheard by Theseus but heard very clearly by us, is there as a free agent to warn and to guard. He is, in the darkest and deepest sense that the word will bear, the play's enchanter.

As he speaks he can be busy with his broom, but the most magical Puck I have seen was completely still, a small half-naked boy-faun, delivering his spell in a timeless moment. In such a way of playing, the pronouncement of Puck's blessing – 'Not a mouse/Shall disturb this hallowed house' – has an eerie atmospheric power which blends pagan and Christian echoes in a magical unity.

The other fairies then appear, and a fuller action resumes: appropriately for this play, the action of the dance and of music. This is the physical ordering of supernatural grace. As it proceeds, the act of blessing which began with Puck is taken over by Titania and Oberon.

All the happy completions that the play's disorders have delayed and predicted now receive their final ceremonious voicing: marriage, fertility, procreation, children, love. They all receive their blessing from the world of nature, of flowers and water, where the fairies live. The reminders of death in Puck's speech are counterbalanced by the reiterated 'ever' of Oberon's. The doubling of time with timelessness which the play introduced in the voice of Theseus, as he spoke to Hermia of growing, living and dying, is finally transmuted into the immortal presences of Oberon and Puck, and made secure.

At last Puck is left alone to speak the epilogue – and what an epilogue! So much of its usual repertoire of conventions and responses has been comically disbarred already, and we are left with lines which, even while they formally speak the expected apology, actually challenge us to be other and more than Theseus, to let the play recede but also to admit its truth:

> If we shadows have offended,
> Think but this, and all is mended:
> That you have but slumbered here
> While these visions did appear.
> And this weak and idle theme,
> No more yielding but a dream,
> Gentles, do not reprehend.
>   (V.i.413–19)

But the idea of the offended audience is a joke, ruled out by the mechanicals. Theseus has already said 'The best in this kind are but shadows', and Puck is the shadow of a shadow, the actor of a night-spirit, yet has now more substance than the world of daylight. We may 'think' or 'imagine' we have slumbered, but we know that in truth we have not; we have been wide awake in the magic of theatrical dream. Again, in this last speech, the much-used word 'dream' is matched with the rarer one, 'vision', and the empty illusion of the first is set in possibility against the transcendental insight of the second. *A Midsummer Night's Dream* will fade and recede like any play, but without forfeiting its truth. In answer to Puck's challenge we can only say with Sir Thomas Wyatt, 'It was no dream; I lay broad waking'.

And indeed the imaginative challenge, the choice of truths, is not between the sleeping dream and the waking dream. We have been awake throughout, just as the 'shadows' we have watched were wide awake when anything of memorable consequence happened to them. The choice is really between the wideawake dream and the vision, the first perhaps illusory and treacherous even if a conscious thing, the second an insight into hidden but significant truth.

Caroline Spurgeon noted of *A Midsummer Night's Dream*:

No wonder Keats underscored this play almost continuously, for sheer poetry, nature and moonlight were his lovers, and he found them all here together to his hand, as nowhere else in literature, in rich and joyous abundance. And these, largely through the imagery ... have stamped their special impress on the play, which leaves us, as it has left myriads ... amazed and bewitched by beauty and the strange power of the poet's pen.

(*Shakespeare's Imagery*, p. 263)

It is Keats who should be given the last word, and credited with the indirect utterance of the most essential critical observation on the play. The closing scene and Puck's epilogue do not *assert* the play's alternative truth, but they ask the question which contains the mystery. The scene and the play leave us in the half-light of uncertainty for one brief moment, exactly where we saw Bottom and the lovers in their own awakening, recessive moments in Act IV. Keats phrased perfectly the question for that final moment of dramatic half-light, in the closing lines of the 'Ode to a Nightingale',

> Was it a vision, or a waking dream?
> Fled is that music – Do I wake or sleep?

Further Reading

Editions

Throughout this study the edition primarily used is the New Penguin, edited by Stanley Wells, which is recommended. All quotations and line-references relate to this edition. Also useful is the Arden Shakespeare edition, edited by Harold F. Brooks, which has a much more substantial editorial apparatus. This edition, though strong in other ways, is not much concerned with the play on the stage. In this respect, but in no other, the New Cambridge edition, edited by R. A. Foakes, improves upon it. There is helpful material in the Signet edition, edited by Wolfgang Clemen.

Wells, Stanley (ed.), *A Midsummer Night's Dream*, New Penguin Shakespeare (Harmondsworth, 1967)

Brooks, Harold F. (ed.), *A Midsummer Night's Dream*, The Arden Shakespeare (London, 1979)

Clemen, Wolfgang (ed.), *A Midsummer Night's Dream*, Signet Shakespeare (New York, 1963)

Foakes, R. A. (ed.), *A Midsummer Night's Dream*, New Cambridge Shakespeare (Cambridge, 1984)

Criticism and Background

A number of studies listed below are reprinted, in whole or in part, in *Shakespeare, A Midsummer Night's Dream: A Casebook* edited by Antony W. Price (Macmillan Education, London, 1983), an extremely useful and readily accessible collection of critical views.

The two items asterisked are concise and helpful reviews of modern critical writing on early Shakespearean comedy, including *A Midsummer Night's Dream*.

Barber, C. L., *Shakespeare's Festive Comedy: A Study of Dramatic Form and Its Relation to Social Custom* (Princeton, NJ, 1959)

Berry, Ralph, *Shakespeare's Comedies: Explorations in Form* (Princeton, NJ, 1972)

Bradbrook, M. C., *Shakespeare and Elizabethan Poetry* (London, 1951)

Briggs, K. M., *The Anatomy of Puck: An Examination of Fairy Beliefs among Shakespeare's Contemporaries and Successors* (London, 1959)

Brown, John Russell, *Shakespeare and his Comedies* (London, 2nd Edn, 1962)

Bullough, Geoffrey, *Narrative and Dramatic Sources of Shakespeare, Vol. 1: Early Comedies, Poems, 'Romeo and Juliet'* (London, 1957)

Calderwood, James L., '*A Midsummer Night's Dream*: the Illusion of Drama', *Modern Language Quarterly* 26 (1965), pp. 506–22, reprinted in *Shakespearean Metadrama* (Minneapolis, 1971)

Carroll, William C., *The Metamorphoses of Shakespearean Comedy* (Princeton, NJ, 1985)

Charlton, H. B., *Shakespearian Comedy* (London, 1938)

Cope, Jackson I., *The Theatre and the Dream: From Metaphor to Form in Renaissance Drama* (Baltimore, 1973)

*Danson, Lawrence, 'Twentieth-century Shakespeare Criticism: The Comedies' in Stanley Wells (ed.) *The Cambridge Companion to Shakespeare Studies* (Cambridge, 1986)

Dent, R. W., 'Imagination in *A Midsummer Night's Dream*', *Shakespeare Quarterly* XV (1964), pp. 115–29

Evans, Bertrand, *Shakespeare's Comedies* (London, 1960)

Fender, Stephen, *Shakespeare: A Midsummer Night's Dream* (London, 1968)

Frye, Northrop, 'The Argument of Comedy' in Leonard F. Dean (ed.) *Shakespeare: Modern Essays in Criticism* (New York, 2nd Edn, 1967)

Garber, Marjorie B., *Dreams in Shakespeare* (New Haven, 1974)

Granville-Barker, Harley, *Prefaces to Shakespeare*, First Series (London, 1927)

Hamilton, A. C., *The Early Shakespeare* (San Marino, 1967)

Hunter, G. K., *William Shakespeare: The Late Comedies*, British Council 'Writers and their Work' series (London, 1962)

Hunter, G. K., *John Lyly: The Humanist as Courtier* (London, 1962)

Kermode, Frank, 'The Mature Comedies' in J. R. Brown and B. Harris (eds.) *Early Shakespeare* (London, 1961)

Knight, G. Wilson, *The Shakespearean Tempest* (London, 1932)

Kott, Jan, *Shakespeare Our Contemporary* (London, 1964)

Latham, Minor White, *The Elizabethan Fairies* (New York, 1930)

Leggatt, Alexander, *Shakespeare's Comedy of Love* (London, 1974)

McGuire, Philip C., *Speechless Dialect: Shakespeare's Open Silences* (Berkeley, 1985)

Miller, Ronald F., '*A Midsummer Night's Dream*: The Fairies, Bottom, and the Mystery of Things', *Shakespeare Quarterly* XXVI (1975), pp. 254–68

Muir, Kenneth (ed.), *Shakespeare Survey 24* (Cambridge, 1971)
See the articles 'A Necessary Theatre' by Peter Thomson and 'Free Shakespeare' by John Russell Brown, on Peter Brook's celebrated and controversial 1970 production of the play. Compare also with the discussion by Roger Warren, listed below.

Muir, Kenneth, '*Pyramus and Thisbe*: A Study in Shakespeare's Method', *Shakespeare Quarterly* V (1954), pp. 141–53

Nevo, Ruth, *Comic Transformations in Shakespeare* (London, 1980)

Olson, Paul A., '*A Midsummer Night's Dream* and the Meaning of Court Marriage', *Journal of English Literary History* 24 (1957), pp. 95–119

*Palmer, D. J., 'The Early Comedies' in Stanley Wells (ed.) *Shakespeare: A Bibliographical Guide* (Oxford, 1990)

Pettet, E. C., *Shakespeare and the Romance Tradition* (London, 1949)

Phialas, Peter G., *Shakespeare's Romantic Comedies* (Chapel Hill, NC, 1966)

Price, Antony W. (ed.), *Shakespeare, A Midsummer Night's Dream: A Casebook* (London, 1983)

Salingar, Leo, *Shakespeare and the Traditions of Comedy* (Cambridge, 1974)

Schanzer, Ernest, 'The Moon and the Fairies in *A Midsummer Night's Dream*', *University of Toronto Quarterly* XXIV (1955)

Siegel, Paul N., '*A Midsummer Night's Dream* and the Wedding Guests', *Shakespeare Quarterly* IV (1953), pp. 139–44

Thompson, Ann, *Shakespeare's Chaucer: A Study in Literary Origins* (Liverpool, 1978)

Warren, Roger, *A Midsummer Night's Dream: Text and Performance* (London, 1983)

Wells, Stanley, '*A Midsummer Night's Dream* Revisited', *Critical Survey* III i (1991)

Young, David P., *Something of Great Constancy: The Art of 'A Midsummer Night's Dream'* (New Haven, 1966)